SUCCESSFUL GR

FAMILY REFERENCE

SUCCESSFUL GRANDPARENTING

How to manage family relationships
and practical issues

Doris Corti

" GROWING INTO THE ROLE "

How To Books

Cartoons by Mike Flanagan

British Library Cataloguing in Publication Data
A catalogue record for this book is available from the British Library.

© Copyright 1997 by Doris Corti.

First published in 1997 by How To Books Ltd, 3 Newtec Place,
Magdalen Road, Oxford OX4 1RE, United Kingdom.
Tel: (01865) 793806. Fax: (01865) 248780.

Note: The material contained in this book is set out in good faith for
general guidance and no liability can be accepted for loss or expense
incurred as a result of relying in particular circumstances on statements
made in the book. The laws and regulations are complex and liable to
change, and readers should check the current position with the relevant
authorities before making personal arrangements.

Produced for How To Books by Deer Park Productions.
Typeset by PDQ Typesetting, Stoke-on-Trent, Staffs.
Printed and bound by Cromwell Press, Broughton Gifford, Melksham,
Wiltshire.

Contents

List of Illustrations

Preface

Becoming a grandparent can be an exciting new venture. It can also be a time when there are extra worries and problems. Today, many grandparents assist in the upbringing of their grandchildren. This may entail assisting financially as well as in other practical ways. There are always difficulties, but careful thought and planning can help to overcome many of these. It is hoped that this book will not only help those who are daunted by the thought of becoming a grandparent for the first time but also help solve some of the problems even the most experienced of grandparents may encounter along the way.

In today's society some of the difficulties which beset many families seem insurmountable, but the courage displayed by those I have spoken to disproves this. This book is for them; they are a testimony to successful grandparenting.

I am indebted to my local library, and to the many individuals, organisations and societies who have supplied me with information, as well as various illustrations and leaflets. Their assistance has been invaluable in achieving my aim: to help grandparents in every aspect of grandparenting.

Doris Corti

This book can help you...

- [ ] Prepare to become a grandparent
- [ ] Know where to turn for professional advice
- [ ] Learn how to play a supporting role
- [ ] Help with the problems of one parent families
- [ ] Track down useful organisations
- [ ] Entertain the grandchildren successfully
- [ ] Form good relationships with teenage grandchildren
- [ ] Practise diplomacy within the family
- [ ] Learn how to be an effective listener
- [ ] Give really practical help when needed
- [ ] Give constructive advice to grandchildren
- [ ] Come to terms with a new family
- [ ] Provide much needed reassurance
- [ ] Enjoy the role of grandparenting to the full
- [ ] Become a successful step-grandparent
- [ ] Give the right kind of financial help
- [ ] Offer your experience of looking after young children
- [ ] Cope successfully with family holidays
- [ ] Help out with accommodation
- [ ] Keep in touch
- [ ] Discover how to live successfully with another generation

1
Preparing to be a Grandparent

Grandparents always were, and still can be, part of family life, although they have changed from their original image. They often lead far busier lives than they did in the past, and many are holding down demanding jobs, as well as running a home.

The general overview of the family is that it has changed a great deal. What used to be considered a family unit – a husband, wife and children – cannot now be taken for granted. Life expectancy is greater, so in all probability you will be grandparents for a long time. Changes occur in family life through divorce, one-parent families, marriages (or partnerships) of mixed cultures, as well as step-families. Grandparents nowadays are learning how to adapt to different family needs.

This chapter offers advice about the following:

- your role as a grandparent
- when to seek professional advice
- playing a supporting role
- offering practical help.

DISCUSSING YOUR ROLE

When you first learn that you are to become a grandparent, you are excited, and probably a little apprehensive. This is a new part of your life, and one with which you may not be familiar. You will perhaps, want to talk to the prospective parents and find out if they have any worries or problems that you think you can help them with. These may be minor or major ones. Whatever way you think you can assist try to discuss these fully to arrive at the best decision for all concerned.

Ways you can help
Other members of the family, and friends, may want to assist the expectant parents or parent, and you, as new grandparents should

try to be diplomatic as well as helpful. Asking how you can help will show that you are *willing* to provide assistance, whilst at the same time not being pushy. Discussing ways of helping with the parents can bring mutual satisfaction. Three ways you can offer help are:

* financially
* on a personal basis
* help with accommodation.

Providing financial help

Financial help can be given by opening a bank or savings account for the baby. If a large amount is to be invested, perhaps for a child's future education, it is wise to consult a financial adviser to ensure that you benefit from any possible tax relief. Most banks have a consultant who will give you advice. Another way to help financially, is by offering to buy costly items such as the pram, cot or baby clothing.

Providing personal help

There are several ways in which you could offer help during the time of pregnancy. Looking after other children in the family, or accompanying the expectant mother on hospital or clinic visits provides practical assistance. Your willingness to discuss other ways of helping after the new baby's arrival will also be valued. These may include babysitting or if the mother intends to return to work after the baby's birth, then your help in childminding might also be needed.

Helping with accommodation

Help with accommodation may be offered in several ways. Nowadays many young couples and single parents are living on state benefits. Often the accommodation they are in is unsuitable to return to after the baby is born. Worrying as this may be for you, the grandparents, it is best not to rush into any arrangement until you have discussed the problems with the parent(s) of the baby. The possible ways you could help are by:

* offering accommodation in your own home
* contacting the local housing authority
* offering to help pay the rent.

Don't forget that young people like to be independent. Let them know that you are willing to help, but allow a little time for them to manage their own affairs. Using tact at this point may be a way of resolving past problems or quarrels, as well as avoiding new ones.

SEEKING PROFESSIONAL ADVICE

Sometimes it is necessary to seek professional advice in order to fulfil your role as a grandparent. Fortunately today, there are many organisations and services, both voluntary and state sponsored that can assist you. These include:

- Citizens Advice Bureau (CAB)
- Grandparents' Federation
- The Family Rights Group.

Making a will
You may need to make a will, especially if you have decided to leave an amount of money for your grandchildren. Your local Citizens Advice Bureau can help you to locate a solicitor who will then advise you on the necessary procedure. Your CAB will also be able to give advice on such matters as housing and supply you with the relevant addresses to write to.

Getting legal advice
Separation or divorce can create bitterness within a whole family relationship. It may be necessary therefore, for grandparents who are denied access to their grandchildren to obtain legal advice.

In 1989 The Children Act was implemented, and grandparents are now allowed to ask leave of the court to apply for reasonable contact. (This is even if the parents of the child, or children, do not approve.) The court will then decide if such contact is in the child's or children's best interest.

Resolving disputes
Disputes can arise over custodianship, and access rights. The Grandparents' Federation is a national organisation that gives advice and support to grandparents who have young relatives 'in care'. This Federation was formed in 1987 and was the brainchild of the Family Rights Group. The Grandparents' Federation, together with other organisations and individuals, has worked to achieve a change in child care laws.

Knowing where to turn
If you should have any problems with regard to *eg* access rights, remember that you are not alone. There are various organisations that will offer you support and advice.

- The Grandparents' Federation can supply a list of solicitors who are qualified to help grandparents in difficult circumstances.

- The Family Rights Group has a support network for grandparents of children in the care of local authorities. Legal advice may be obtained through them.

- Contact centres have been set up in some areas to help where a parent is proving unreasonable in allowing the other parent to see or communicate with a child or children.

In some areas members of The Mothers Union, which is a Church of England voluntary organisation, are willing to sit in, quite unobtrusively, (or be near at hand) in Contact centres, to enable a parent to see a child or children without distress. Such meeting places can bring peace of mind to parents and grandparents alike.

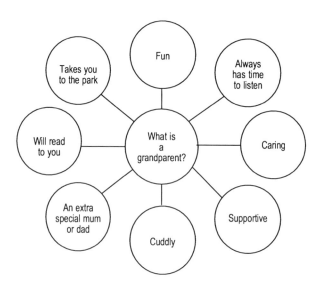

Fig. 1. What is a grandparent?

PLAYING A SUPPORTING ROLE

'Grandparents are extra mums and dads' is one way the extended family was described by a seven-year-old to his teacher. See Figure 1 which perhaps sums up how children see the role of a grandparent. The caring that grandparents give is invaluable. As mentioned earlier you may be able to help financially, as well as being someone to turn to as a companion during hospital visits if a need arises. There are however, so many ways in which you can give your support.

Example

When Karen was having her first child she developed some complications and had to have further blood tests. 'I'm a bit scared', she confided to her mother, who had a full-time job. 'Don't worry', was the immediate response, and her mother then arranged to take all her holiday entitlement. 'So that I can come with you when you have those tests', she explained to Karen. Thankfully, the tests proved that there was nothing seriously wrong. Until then Karen had thought that her mother's job took priority over everything. After the birth of her son, she had a better relationship with her mother.

Knowing how to give support

You may be able to give practical support in ways that are obvious. For instance, if a child is ill or has to stay in hospital, your help will be invaluable in getting meals and doing shopping. If there are other children in the family you might be needed to take them to and from school. If the mother stays in hospital with a sick child, you may find it suits everyone better if the siblings stay with you during this time.

Providing reassurance

You can create a supportive atmosphere by staying calm during a crisis. Listening to a child's worries about the illness their brother or sister may have, can bring them the reassurance they are seeking. Such a time is stressful for children. They may be afraid that what is happening to another member of their family, might also happen to them. They remember catching other illnesses like chickenpox or mumps, and may well ask you if they will catch this one too. With mother and father rushing to fit in hospital visits it may fall to you, as a grandparent, to reassure them.

Being the comforter

Comforting is another way of being supportive, and a vital one. You may need to comfort a grandchild when parents are separating, divorcing or if either is ill or dying. You too may be distressed, but your personal feelings will be put aside to help the children who are involved. Just the simple fact that 'Granny' or 'Grandpa' is there for them will be comforting. Even if you can't always be there in person writing and telephoning regularly will let them know you are thinking about them and that still provides valuable support.

Whenever your support is needed it is important to:

- **Be perceptive** – certain things can show that a child is still distressed. Nightmares, and aggressive behaviour are two things that can show that a child is still struggling to come to terms with something very difficult to understand.

- **Listen** – let a child tell you of their fears and their worries. Talking about the person who has died is very important, and fortunately nowadays, death is not a taboo subject.

Your unconditional love will be the most important thing that you can give at this time.

Remember, however, that being supportive does not mean that your own interests have to be discarded. Even if you give these up for a while to help out, hopefully you need not give them up altogether.

Example

Moira and John had a hobby of collecting china and glass antiques, and were quite knowledgeable on the subject. When they retired they toured the antique fairs, setting up their stall and delighting in a new way of life. They made new friends but still found time to give support to their family. When their six-year-old grandson had to undergo an operation, they looked after the younger children, and were on hand whenever they were needed.

Example

Jean was concerned that she did not portray a true grandmotherly image to her daughters when they had babies. This was because in her retirement she had started a small publishing business that kept her fully occupied. Both daughters told her: 'We'd rather have you happy. Carry on with your life mum, we know you'd help out in an emergency.' Jean did just that when her eldest daughter had to have a caesarean section performed. She switched dates, postponed meetings, and rearranged her days to assist. As 'grandma' she was much needed at this time, and afterwards.

OFFERING PRACTICAL HELP

Nowadays many young mums need to go to work. One way of offering practical help is to volunteer to mind the children on a regular basis. They might be at school most of the day, but need to be met and looked after until their mother comes home. If however, you have a grandchild or children to look after during the day keeping them occupied can be very demanding.

- Take them out to parks, shops and areas of interest.

- When the weather is bad and you are tied to the house make sure you have lots of books suitable for their age groups. Keep plenty of plain paper for drawing and writing on, as well as pencils and coloured crayons.

- Keep a large assortment of soft toys, dolls, dolls' clothes, model-making kits, toy cars, jigsaws, board games. Children love to dress up, so hang on to any old clothes.

Conserving energy

Little children can be fun, but exhausting. If there are two of you looking after them, take it in turns to each have a short break during the day. You may also find it difficult to fit in your routine household chores. With lively children around everything can take double the time.

- Keep chores to a minimum.

- Get the children to help! Make up a rota with your names and the children's on. Have a coloured wall chart listing names, dates and what jobs need to be done. Let them strike out each job on the chart as it is finished and make sure you give praise when it is due.

- When the weather is fine enough the chart can be used for tackling small chores in the garden (or jobs like cleaning shoes *etc*, if you have no garden).

- Make sure you change individual jobs around, so that no one gets resentful about always doing one particular job.

Helping the anxious parent

Parents may be anxious about leaving young children, even if it is for short periods. They may need reassurance to start with. Whether your help is required on a temporary or more permanent basis the fact that you show you are *willing* to assist in *some* way will make the parents feel comfortable asking you.

Minding children during illness

If you are minding younger members of a family where someone is ill, it is important to:

- Answer any questions they may put to you about the illness.

- Keep them occupied and amused.

- Let them think they are helping you, rather than the other way round!

- Encourage your grandchildren to talk to you about their day at school, or elsewhere. Keep their lives as normal as possible.

Taking care of yourself

With any illness, considerable strain is placed on those who are caring for the sick person, whether this is a child or an adult. You may perhaps be called upon to help in a more physical capacity than you are used to. You may be walking more, standing waiting for buses and trains and lifting and carrying more. Apart from the extra physical strain, the mental effort of keeping a cheerful face on things in front of other members of the family can be exhausting. Make sure you:

- rest when you can
- eat properly
- have a good night's rest whenever possible
- ask other relatives or friends to help when you feel particularly exhausted.

Organising willing helpers

Other relatives and friends may *want* to help. Avoid friction in a family by:

- discussing the situation
- keeping a note of dates and times when other relatives or friends can give help

- not quarrelling over who will mind the grandchildren in the event of a crisis.

CASE STUDIES

George and Margaret help out

George and Margaret were well off and so had planned to travel round the world visiting friends and relatives when they retired. However, their daughter-in-law became seriously ill and died, leaving their son Brian to cope with two small children. George and Margaret put aside their plans, and took the children (Robert aged seven, and Karen aged five) to live with them. Brian, who had his own accountancy business, provided financially for the children and had them home at weekends and during the holidays.

Two years after his wife's death, Brian married a divorcee with two young boys and so Robert and Karen went back to live with them. However, they did not settle quickly and Brian's new wife decided that they had been spoilt by their grandparents. She thought it best if they did not contact the children again.

Although distressed, George and Margaret agreed. The only way they could see their grandchildren was by watching them when they passed their house on the way to and from school. George decided to get legal advice, but before he could do so Brian had a heart attack. It was not serious but he was kept in hospital for tests. George telephoned the new wife offering help. She was glad of this, as her own parents lived in Spain. George and Margaret looked after all four children and their relationship with their new daughter-in-law improved. They helped out generally, and with his business acumen George was able to keep affairs in order for his son's firm. Brian's recovery was speeded up by the knowledge that family relationships were so improved, and Margaret was heard telling a friend 'and we have two step-grandchildren as well now!'

Contacts who helped Jane and Scott

Jane and her partner Scott, both unemployed, were struggling to bring up their three-year-old son. Their small flat was damp, and the local housing authority promised to rehouse them, but there was a long waiting list. The stress of their financial situation, combined with the fact that Scott was a heavy drinker, caused problems. They quarrelled a lot, and finally parted after Scott hit Jane during an argument.

Jane returned to live with her mother, taking Paul, their young son with her. Scott, who was trying to stop drinking, wanted to see his son, but Jane was unwilling to agree to this.

The grandmother realised that they needed specialised legal help to deal with the problems arising. The Citizens Advice Bureau gave her the name of a solicitor qualified to give them the assistance they needed. Jane is relieved to know that whatever develops in the future between her and Scott and their son, she will have the expertise of a professional to guide her.

Giving Kim some help

Kim, a single parent with a two-year-old daughter, needed help when she was involved in a horrendous road accident. She lay in a coma for several weeks. During this time her widowed mother looked after the little girl. Kim recovered but was partially disabled, and unable to continue her high-powered job as a personal assistant to the director of an international company.

When Kim was finally discharged from hospital social services decided that because of her disability, she would not be able to look after her daughter for some time. They also considered the grandparent too old to continue to mind the child. An order was made to place the little girl in care. A foster home was found and to begin with this worked well. However, Kim became depressed, both over her continuing disability and at the loss of her child. She deteriorated and needed psychiatric help.

At this time, the decision was made to place the child in a children's home for a year. Kim's mother was worried about whether she would be denied access to her grandchild. She heard about the Grandparents' Federation and contacted them. She was given advice about both her own and Kim's legal position and visiting rights.

When Kim recovered, it was agreed that with continuing help her daughter could once again live with her.

DISCUSSION POINTS

1. What is the best way you think you can help your grandchildren?

2. What organisations can give you the professional advice you need?

3. In what ways could you give valuable support to your family?

4. What name would you like to be known by as a grandparent?

5. How do you feel about looking after your small grandchildren all day?

2
Growing into the Role

In this chapter we will discuss the following:

- how you can enjoy being a grandparent
- sharing memories
- when to give advice
- how to create opportunities to help
- helping with older grandchildren
- avoiding conflict in the family.

ENJOYING BEING A GRANDPARENT

Being a grandparent may not come naturally. It can however, bring a great deal of pleasure. Here are some of the ways:

- gaining a sense of purpose in later life
- receiving companionship
- sharing children's problems
- having fun with the family.

Example: Rita finds a sense of purpose again

Rita was lonely after her husband died. She filled in time by joining retirement clubs and various committees but none of these brought her any satisfaction. Her daughter and family live nearby, but although they telephoned regularly, they were always too busy to visit her as much as she would have liked.

However, Rita's life changed when her eldest grandson Sam, was fourteen. He and his mother weren't getting on and she was at her wit's end. Rita suggested to her desperate daughter that Sam stayed with her over the long school holidays. They got on well and he was able to talk to his grandmother about his feelings and ambitions. When term began he remained with Rita on the understanding that he kept in contact with his parents. Although Rita had doubts about it at first, it worked well for both of them. Sam took over her garden, which had been a complete wilderness since her husband died. He settled back into school work and decided on a career in horticulture. He eventually began to spend longer at home with his parents but continued to pop in on Rita every day. Sam had given her a sense of purpose, and she felt rejuvenated.

Example: Howard finds companionship

After taking early retirement Howard, a divorcee, missed his friends at the office and found that the hours dragged. He suggested to his two daughters and son, who were all married with families, that he organise and pay for excursions and holidays. During the year Howard arranged that each set of grandchildren in turn visited him. He organised cinema and theatre outings, as well as various trips. This brought him the companionship he missed, especially as sometimes a grandchild would ask if they could bring a friend!

Solving problems

Teenagers, particularly, brood on their problems. There are many pressures on teenagers today, both from their contemporaries, in the form of peer pressure (*eg* to try drugs) and from society at large, as well as all the usual worries that arise in adolescence. It is important to create an atmosphere in which your grandchildren will feel they can come to you and talk about their problems in confidence and without being judged. Children will often seek older people and those living outside the home to share their problems with, so as grandparents they could choose **you**.

Always make sure you show an interest in what your grandchildren tell you. They need to feel that you will listen and help them. Make a special effort by:

- taking a grandchild out for a treat when you suspect something is wrong
- remaining calm and reassuring
- thinking of practical ways to solve the problem.

Grandparents can prove themselves to be sympathetic listeners to children of all ages.

Having fun as a grandparent

There are many ways you can enjoy your grandchildren. When they are very young they can bring fun and enjoyment to your lives. You can make sure this happens by:

- seizing opportunities to babysit or take children out when asked
- playing with them and their toys.

Every stage of a child's development is fascinating. Getting to know a child by babysitting, going out for a walk with them, or simply playing with their dolls and trains *etc* can prove to be fun. A simple board or card game can produce much laughter.

Being fun for older grandchildren
What can you do about having fun when children are older?

- Talk about fashion. Teenagers are very clothes-conscious. Admire your granddaughter's hairstyle and make-up. Tell your grandson how much his 'trendy' appearance suits him.

- Listen to their choice of music and try to learn the names of their favourite singers, groups *etc*. Chat with them about these.

- Take pride in your grandchildren's achievements in any sport. Your hearty cheers during a rugby or football match, at a swimming gala, or elsewhere will be appreciated. These events and school sportsdays can be lots of fun.

What if you don't live near enough to join in such activities?

- Write to, or telephone your grandchildren. Keep informed about their hobbies. It's fun looking for birthday and Christmas gifts relating to your grandchildren's interests.

Advantages and disadvantages of being a grandparent

Advantages	*Disadvantages*
Companionship	Asked to babysit too often
Acquiring a sense of purpose again	Extra expenditure
	Life dominated by children again
Time to talk and play with your grandchildren (which you didn't always have with your children)	You may have to change your lifestyle
Grandchildren return home so that you can rest!	

SHARING MEMORIES

Talking with grandchildren

The conversations that you have with your grandchildren will be part of their memories. You, as grandparents, bring a sense of continuity to children of whatever age. The gap in generations can often enhance a family relationship, and work extremely well.

When talking to your grandchildren remember the following points:

1. Comment in a sincere way.

2. Do not laugh at a teenage grandchild's clothes or their hairstyle, or the way they look in any way.

3. Do discuss items of clothing and other things, sensibly, and without making your grandchild feel self-conscious.

Example
Granddad was staying in his granddaughter's home. He badly needed a haircut but was waiting until he went home again. 'Here, borrow my hair gel,' young William offered. Granddad accepted the offer and a conversation developed about whether granddad preferred the gel to his usual hair cream. William felt grown-up because he'd persuaded Granddad to change his hair toiletry, while Granddad felt part of the 'young scene' because William had bothered to lend him the gel.

It's these little snippets of conversations that make a difference. The confidences about school, or girl or boyfriends, and about home that grandparents are most likely to have firsthand news of.

Keeping the past alive
The past appears to fascinate young children. There are some things they cannot comprehend and perhaps only read of or see on television. Talk about these things with your grandchildren. Tell them about:

- what your schooldays were like
- the clothes you wore
- your experience of war
- the first car you had
- what the house where you grew up was like.

Keeping in touch
You or your grandchildren may live overseas. Keep the conversations going by letters, tapes and photographs. Send pictures of where you have been and what you have been doing. You may not always get a prompt reply (or any) but *you* will be talking to *them*, and **they will remember**.

So, if you live far away from your grandchildren here are some suggestions for keeping in touch:

1. Send them letters that are newsy, and chatty.

2. Send them tapes telling them about some of the interesting things you've been doing/reading, *etc.*

3. Send them photographs of yourself, or of places you have visited, your garden, holiday snaps *etc.*

4. Write about the new car, or how the old one is doing.

5. Tell your grandchildren if you have joined a new club, or taken up a new hobby.

Talking about the present
Of course, it would be unwise to talk merely about the past. It would get boring for your grandchildren and you need to be a **vital** part of the family. So keep abreast of the topics that your grandchildren are interested in and like to talk about. These will vary according to their ages of course. Daytime television programmes have introduced several characters into toddlers' lives. You can learn about these and your small granddaughter or grandson will be delighted to keep you informed. Older grandchildren may be away from home, and possibly will not write to you. However, you can keep in touch by:

- remembering their birthdays
- sending a small gift or some money as a treat occasionally
- writing a card if you go away on holiday.

Keeping these lines of communication open is all important. If you do this, then your grandchildren will be relaxed in your company when you do meet again.

ADVISING WHEN ASKED

It can be difficult to give advice, but if asked make sure you get the correct information.

Discussing education
Contact your local Education Authority for details regarding schools, and the catchment area your family are in. Enquire about nursery schools, as well as infant, primary and secondary schools that come within your family's area. Check whether there is a bus route or train service that is convenient for the school selected.

Private schools
A list of names can be obtained from your local Education Authority.

Health matters

Make sure that your grandchildren are registered with a GP. Details of GPs and the services they offer are available in Community Health Council offices and in all public libraries.

Answering their questions

You may be asked for advice by your grandchildren themselves. Right from a very young child's plea of 'Granddad, Mummy says you always tell the truth, please tell me if there is a real Father Christmas?' Or, you could receive a letter from an older child like the example in Figure 2 from a confused 19-year-old granddaughter.

Sometimes the generation gap can be an advantage when things like this need to be discussed calmly. The experience gathered over the years can prove helpful.

There are numerous ways your advice will be sought. Sometimes it may be difficult, but careful thought and the correct information, as well as your understanding will always prove valuable.

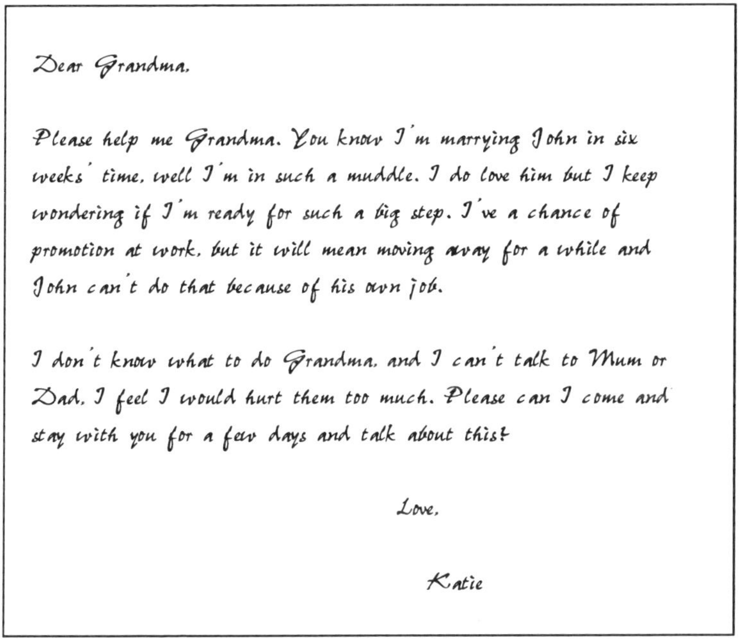

Dear Grandma,

Please help me Grandma. You know I'm marrying John in six weeks' time, well I'm in such a muddle. I do love him but I keep wondering if I'm ready for such a big step. I've a chance of promotion at work, but it will mean moving away for a while and John can't do that because of his own job.

I don't know what to do Grandma, and I can't talk to Mum or Dad. I feel I would hurt them too much. Please can I come and stay with you for a few days and talk about this?

Love,

Katie

Fig. 2. Letter from a confused granddaughter
asking her grandmother's advice.

CREATING OPPORTUNITIES TO HELP

You may find that you need to **create opportunities to help**. Your grandchildren may be self-sufficient, and their parents independent. You will, as grandparents still want to assist them, even when there does not appear to be any obvious way to do so. Giving money to your grandchildren, or putting it aside for their future may be a way of helping. However, always make sure that the parents approve of this sort of help.

Helping financially

Opening a young savers' account
Most banks operate some sort of scheme for young savers (*ie* children aged ten and under). The account is normally opened in the child's name but a grown-up can open it on their behalf. Contact the bank of your choice to obtain details.

National savings
This is another way of giving financial help to your grandchildren. Money can be put aside in the form of children's bonds, capital bonds, as well as investment and ordinary accounts.

Building societies and insurance companies
By opening an account for your grandchild with a building society you are again creating an opportunity to help financially. There are several accounts to choose from and its is worth shopping around. With some insurance companies you can invest with bonds, and depending on the company and the amount involved, annual and lump sum options are available.

Finding other ways to help
You may find you can create areas where you can help more practically. You may for example, think that one of your grand-children is feeling 'left out' of things. It may be because a new baby has arrived in the family, or a stepbrother or sister is sharing their home. Whatever the problem, you will be able to help them through this difficult time in a number of ways.

Treat each child fairly
It is important to demonstrate to your grandchildren that one isn't favoured above the others.

- Have all the children round to your home together when possible. This shows that you are not favouring one more than another. Don't take sides in an argument. Stay calm and be supportive.

- If you live too far away to have children home then create a pattern of helping regularly through chatting on the phone. If you send money or presents through the post send something to all of them. This token gesture of affection will not be forgotten.

Make sure you talk to older children about the situation. The following case study illustrates how valuable this can be.

Janet explains her viewpoint
Janet was upset when she saw her ten-year-old grandson Mark, becoming withdrawn. He refused to join in any activities with Kevin, his stepbrother. He loved sports but wouldn't go to any of his favourite games if Kevin was going. He argued with his parents a lot.

Janet said: 'He'd always stayed one night a week with me at my house, and continued to do so. One night I told him how difficult it was for me to have a new grandson in the family but that it was not fair to leave him out of family arrangements, or make him feel unwanted. I suggested that next time Mark came to stay with me that he bring Kevin, so that we could get to know each other better. It took a little while for this to happen but they both come now, and get on much better at home. Mark has stopped arguing so much with his parents too.'

QUESTIONS AND ANSWERS

My granddaughter is upset because her mother who is divorced has remarried. As well as a new father she how has to accept a stepsister. How can I help her come to terms with this?

Take every opportunity to explain that you too, are finding this a difficult time. This may help your granddaughter to understand that the change it affecting everyone in the family. Keep to a firm rule about treating all the children equally. Remain patient, and do not take sides in any family quarrels.

I do not have a large income but other relatives who do, are able to buy my grandsons expensive presents. How can I compete with this?

Try not to think of this as competing. Take time to find out what your grandsons' main interests are. For example, a roll of film for the expensive cameras they may possess, or blank tapes for them to record favourite music on are all gifts that will be appreciated. Otherwise they would have to buy them out of their own pocket-money. Some gifts you might be able to make yourself, using your talents. A personal touch will be valued.

My four-year-old granddaughter Jessie, is jealous of her new baby brother. She has become very clingy and cries over small upsets. How can I help?

If you pass a complementary comment on the new baby make sure you praise Jessie also. This way she will know that your feelings for her are still as strong. For instance, if you take a small gift for the baby, make sure that you take one for Jessie too. Tell her the gift is because she is helping Mummy with the new baby. Praise her when you can, get her to talk to you about her new brother, make her feel important.

HELPING WITH OLDER GRANDCHILDREN

As children grow older their lives become more complex. They may have friends you disapprove of, or they may have some problems that upset them. If your relationship with them has been built on affection and trust, they will know that they can confide in you. Your experience of life can help them through traumatic periods.

Example: Janine finds her grandparents understanding
When Janine was 18 she fell in love with a man ten years older and went to live with him. This man drank heavily and was known to the police for being involved in fights. She would not listen to her parents who begged Janine to give him up. During one bout of drinking he struck Janine. She was shocked and distressed and rushed to her grandparents' house. Understanding how much she loved him they did not condemn him, but persuaded her to think carefully before making her future with him. At first Janine went back to live with this man, but his violence grew worse and once again it was her grandparents who were able to assist her. She stayed with them, and eventually gave the man up altogether.

Helping in other ways
Other ways to help may include:

- Giving a temporary home to a grandchild. This may be helpful when they are starting at college or looking for a job. Your home might be in the right area for them.

But remember the unwritten rules:

- Always be tactful when you offer help. Put the suggestion and give your grandson or granddaughter time to think about it.

- Do not take offence if they refuse your offer of help. They may have other plans that suit them better.

Keeping a confidence
Never divulge anything that a grandchild tells you in confidence. It may be difficult in some instances not to do this. You may feel that you should tell the parents what you know. Explain how you feel to your grandchild, and ask if you can speak about what is concerning you. You may even be able to persuade your grandson or granddaughter to speak to their parents themselves.

Being ready to listen
Being always ready to listen isn't as easy as it sounds. You may feel the problem that a grandchild brings to you is a small one. Remember, it is not small to the child otherwise they would not want to discuss it. Be wise and thankful that your grandchild can communicate with you in this way. The poem in Figure 3 illustrates how important it can be to a child to have a grandparent who is always ready to listen.

Sharing grief
The effects of grief can be bewildering. The loss of a favourite pet might be the first experience your grandchild has of feeling such an emotion. You can be helpful by simply letting them see that you share the experience. The death of a loved one is something they may have to cope with, and again grandparents with their own experiences of grief can help their grandchild come to terms with it. Older children might think they should not cry. Let them know that tears are a normal expression of grief. Allow them time to talk about the person they miss, but encourage them to carry on enjoying their own lives in the usual way.

My Grandmother

Wisp of petunia talc,
and the Monday soap smells
are all part of Grandma's house.

She listens to me, sits quietly,
the brown teapot and cups of tea
part of an afternoon ritual.
She's there when I pop in
and moan about school.

She's there when I tell her
'they think I'm a child'.
She's there for my anger, and sadness,
like the time when my cat died.
I'd cried at home, but Grandma knew
how I still cried inside.

Grandma is my friend,
someone who lends me her time,
She's duvet cuddly, warm and lovely.
I enjoy her!

Fig. 3. A schoolgirl's poem about her grandmother.

AVOIDING CONFLICTS WITHIN THE FAMILY

Conflicts in families, whether large or small, are irritating and exhausting. It may be that you favour one or your grandchildren more than the others. The other children may become aware of this, and resentment and conflict may arise. Of, you may be over-demanding of your grandchildren, and want to see them more often than other relatives can. This again creates conflict. Another area of conflict is when grandparents spoil their grandchildren. A little spoiling is usually accepted by parents, but if you overdo it conflicts can occur, especially when you are asked to stop.

Treating everyone fairly

To make sure you aren't accused of favouring anyone here are some tips:

- Make sure that all your grandchildren receive the same presents, attention and most importantly your cuddles.

- Take the same interest in all your grandchildrens' hobbies, exams, jobs *etc.*

- Never compare, and do not comment if one grandchild obtains a higher success rate in examinations or job than any others in the family.

- Do not take sides in any family arguments.

Learning to be diplomatic

When a grandchild turns to you, saying that their brother (or sister) hit them, teased them, or shouted at them, it is so easy to rush to the defence of the grandchild who is complaining. Unfortunately, in the majority of cases, all that will do is provoke an argument. Family situations like this need to be handled with care and diplomacy. Quarrels do arise between brothers and sisters, but are often short lived, and resolved by the children themselves.

Being in charge

Sometimes, when you are in charge of a child, their naughtiness has to be explained to a parent or parents. If a situation has been particularly stressful, then be diplomatic and let tempers cool a little before talking over what has happened. There may be an occasion when another relative (perhaps another grandparent) is upset by what a child has done. This child may be your favourite, but don't jump to his or her defence until you hear the whole account of what actually happened. Try to:

- listen without commenting

- hear all sides of the story

- avoid making snap decisions about who is right, or who is wrong

- watch and see if the same problem arises again, and try to ascertain the reason.

You may not always be on good terms with other relatives in the family always try however, not to let a clash of opinions take place in front of your grandchildren. You can help to stop this happening by avoiding the following:

- raking up past quarrels

- discussing what you consider to be the bad points in another relative's character

- becoming bitter because on occasions, your grandchild seems to prefer to be with their other grandparents.

Dealing with larger conflicts

There are larger issues that can cause conflicts within families. A recent survey has revealed that one in every five children now lives in a one-parent family. Therefore, because of a broken marriage or relationship, your grandchild may move away to live with the parent who is awarded custody. You may not be given what you consider to be reasonable access to the child. Such a scenario may cause great conflict which, if it continues, can result in the grandchildren becoming very distressed.

A change in a relationship can be another source of conflict. If your son or daughter finds a new partner it can very often be hard to come to terms with. It may be difficult for you to accept that your grandchildren have a new mother or father. Your grandchildren too, will be trying to come to terms with this new situation. This may not be easy for them, especially if they have stepsisters or brothers. They will need your understanding.

Adjusting to change

If the family structure changes you will avoid conflict if you:

1. Give yourself time to adjust to any change in family relationships.

2. Do not discuss your personal likes or dislikes about a new partner, wife or husband, with your grandchildren.

3. Avoid discussing the past or comparing a previous marriage/ relationship with the new one.

4. Accept new step-grandchildren as part of the family, and treat them in the same manner as other grandchildren.

You will strengthen relationships, particularly with your grand-children, if you avoid conflicts within the family structure.

CHECKLIST

- List three ways that you could give help to your grandchildren.

- Would you know where to obtain legal guidance if you were denied access to any of your grandchildren?

- Think of ways in which you can keep in touch with older grandchildren if, and when they leave home.

CASE STUDIES

Bridging the generation gap

Jean was really excited when she heard that her granddaughter Sarah would be going to the university in the city where she lived. She'd kept in touch with her grandchildren, but they lived several miles away, and she was unable to see them as often as she would have liked. She wrote to Sarah suggesting that she come and live with her, at least in her first months at university. 'After all,' she wrote, 'you will be in a strange city, and glad to be near someone you know.'

When Sarah did not reply Jean was hurt. It was Sarah's Dad who came and explained that young people look forward to starting out on what to them, was an adventure. When Sarah started university she lived in halls of residence. She did find time to visit her Grandmother, and the generation gap was bridged.

Resolving conflict

Samantha was only five when her parents divorced. She appeared to settle down to a new routine with her mother and visited both sets of grandparents at fairly frequent intervals. However, both sets of grandparents argued over who should have Samantha during the school holidays when her mother was working. Samantha was present during one particular quarrel and was very upset. She told her mother that she did not want to go to any of her grandparents.

It took over six months for the argument to be resolved, and longer for Samantha to be totally happy with any of her grandparents again. Her trust had to be built up. Fortunately, after that initial argument, the grandparents were mature enough to realise that it was Samantha's happiness that was of primary importance.

Creating a way to help

Sylvia was in her early fifties when her only daughter Karen had a baby boy. The father moved away, and did not contact Karen or the child again. Karen returned to work when the child was still young, and Sylvia looked after her grandson.

When the little boy was three Karen found a better job in another area and so she began a new life. Although she still saw her son, Karen was agreeable when her mother suggested trying to find a more permanent arrangement. Sylvia contacted a solicitor who told her she could apply to have legal custodianship of her grandson. Both parents had to give their consent to this, which they did, after an agency was employed to trace the whereabouts of the father. Sylvia, together with the other grandparents, also gave their written consent.

A social worker was also involved, as Sylvia's home had to be established as suitable for a child to live in. Sylvia and her daughter, together with a social worker were seen in the judge's chambers at the county court. Sylvia was granted legal custodianship, and was relieved that everything had been conducted on a friendly basis.

Talking with grandchildren

Fred is a lively, outgoing 70-year-old. He has a large family, including five grandchildren. He is a natural storyteller and can often be heard describing his boyhood, and army experiences to his grandchildren who are aged from five to fifteen years.

Fred is limited in certain activities as he is confined to a wheelchair for most of the time due to an amputation following a wound he received during the Second World War.

His family often think his storytelling would be interesting for others to read. However, Fred doesn't want to write them down because he prefers to tell them in the old oral tradition. Some of Fred's grandchildren attend a local primary school, and the classes are currently working on a project on growing up in the thirties. Simon, Fred's nine-year-old grandson has told his teacher that his Granddad has lots of stories from this period.

Fred was interested to hear about the project and found old photographs of himself as a child, and some taken later, in his army uniform. He also had medals that he had won for various sports, and some of these were inscribed with 1930's dates. He also had some of the old text books that he'd used whilst at school. Fred took all these to the school one day, and saw the headteacher who was very interested in all Fred had to say. It was arranged for him to come in on a certain day, and talk to some of the children. His visit was a great success and because he was so good at talking to the children, and telling them his stories, he was asked into other schools.

Fred's grandchildren are proud of him, and he says it was because of them that he was confident enough to go into their school in the first place. Now these visits have become an integral part of his life.

DISCUSSION POINTS

1. How could you give help without seeming to interfere?

2. Do you think the advantages of being a grandparent outweigh the disadvantages?

3. Do you find that your grandchildren have given you a sense of purpose in life?

4. If you found your grandchild was doing something you considered to be wrong, would you tell their parents?

5. Do you think you give enough time to your grandchildren?

6. Are you able to relate to your grandchildren about their hobbies, ambitions and aims in life?

"GROWING INTO THE ROLE"

3
Solving Problems

This chapter looks in more detail at some of the problems you may have to face as a grandparent and how you can help to solve them. It will cover the following areas:

- overcoming resentments
- thinking positively
- being a step-grandparent
- coping with separation
- knowing your rights as a grandparent including obtaining access to grandchildren.

OVERCOMING RESENTMENTS

Resentments can flare up in an instant, and can easily cause problems in a family if not thought about carefully.

Example

Jean and Roger had two grandchildren who they looked after whilst their son and daughter-in-law were at work. They were dismayed when the couple divorced, and even more so when their son eventually remarried a divorcee, also with two children. The new wife's parents now took an active part in the upbringing of all the grandchildren, and Jean and Roger felt excluded on many family occasions, and resentments crept into their relationship with the family. It took a great deal of restraint for Jean and Roger not to quarrel. They managed to avoid doing so, remaining pleasant when they did meet the family. It took some time, but now all four grandchildren visit them at regular intervals.

Staying neutral

It should not be forgotten that grandchildren settling in with a new parent (or parents), may also be feeling resentful. There may be many reasons for this: a new voice of authority, or jealousy of stepbrothers and sisters are all very big adjustments for children to make.

It may be difficult for you, faced with the emotional outpourings of a favourite grandchild, not to take sides. Lending an ear, or offering the proverbial shoulder to cry on may be helpful, but you should be careful not to allow the new parent to feel you are:

(a) undermining their authority
(b) encouraging your own grandchildren to talk to you, but excluding your step-grandchildren.

You may not like the partner your son or daughter is living with now. It is possible that you feel you do not like any of your step-grandchildren who are now a part of the family unit. You can overcome such resentments by:

- giving yourself time to adjust to the new family
- avoiding making harsh comments
- hiding your own feelings about personal preferences in front of any of your grandchildren
- accepting that your grandchildren will want to visit their other grandparents
- asking a new parent's advice when buying presents for grand-children.

THINKING POSITIVELY

Thinking positively is important in all aspects of being a grand-parent, or a step-grandparent. It can come as a shock when you learn that you are to become a grandparent. Images of white shawls and carpet slippers may drift in front of you and there's nothing wrong with that, if it's what you want.

However, don't allow this image to become reality if you don't want it to. Grandparents have a different image today. Many of them are still working.

Becoming a grandparent can bring a new dimension to your life. Think positively about your new role by:

- tackling problems that may arise in a practical way
- making plans for the future
- discussing how you can help.

Figure 4 looks at some of the negative as well as the positive sides to being a grandparent. Keep thinking positive though and you'll get the most out of being a grandparent.

BEING A STEP-GRANDPARENT

Unless you have known your step-grandchildren over a period of time you will perhaps, not be prepared for the emotions this extra addition to your family can bring. The new grandchildren may differ very much in appearance, and in personality, from your own grandchildren. Remembering to think positive, you can learn to enjoy your new extended role as a step-grandparent if you work hard at:

- getting to know your step-grandchildren

- helping them to overcome any difficulties they may have in adjusting to their new family life

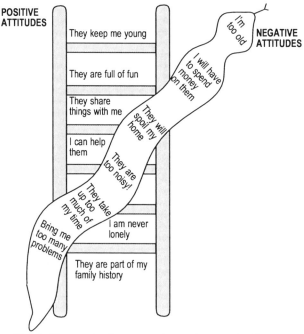

Fig. 4. Your attitude to grandparenting can be like a game of snakes and ladders.

- encouraging all the grandchildren to visit, or keep in touch with you by telephone or letters.

When first meeting your step-grandchildren, and they may be of different ages, treat them naturally. They are now members of your family. If you dislike anything about them (how they dress, talk or look), say nothing. Your comments will achieve nothing positive, and can merely build up resentments. You may of course, find that there are no problems at all about having step-grandchildren, and they are a bonus to your life from the word 'go'.

COPING WITH SEPARATION

In today's unsettled climate of unemployment a family may have to move to another part of the country (or even abroad) for a job. You may be parted from your grandchildren. There are, however, ways to cope with such separation.

- Keeping in constant touch with your grandchildren and family.

- Enjoying your grandchildrens' formative years by having photographs, tapes, and childrens' first drawings sent to you.

- Filling your own life with hobbies and interests. Keep active. Make plans to visit your family and grandchildren. This may be a dream but dreams can sometimes come true.

Separation and sadness
Separation can cause grief. A broken marriage or partnership, or death of a parent can cause suffering, not only to grandparents, but to all the family. Often, a separation cannot be avoided, it can only be coped with and where possible, adjusted to. Sometimes professional counselling can help you through a bad time. You will have friends who may be sympathetic, but to learn how to cope it is advisable to turn to a professionally trained person. You can get advice about counselling from:

- the Samaritans
- your doctor.

Changing names
After separation, the father often worries whether the mother can

An Introduction to:

THE NATIONAL FAMILY TRUST

• Working to enhance and strengthen families in Britain by practical innovations in education, and by family-friendly public policy formation.

• Uniquely, putting prevention first, because it is only common sense to do so. Investment in families saves money, saves tears, saves social unrest.

Fig. 5. Information about The National Family Trust.

WHAT ARE THE TRUST'S EDUCATIONAL ACTIVITIES?

• Urging the recognition of family commitments as essential for personal development and social order. This includes influencing and contributing to the mass media so that constructive family issues gain a higher profile.
• Contributing to conferences and informing change agents in politics, child welfare and teaching.
• Producing an extensive range of educational material – the Life Foundations resource bank – for use with young people and young adults to help them develop into responsible, skilled citizens, family members, and, perhaps, parents.
• Training leaders in techniques for implementing family-related education in a variety of settings.

WHAT DOES THE NATIONAL FAMILY TRUST NEED NOW?

Most of all more **friends**, who will actively support our work by a regular or occasional donation, by offering skilled help, by sponsorship of specific endeavours, or by using and helping to disseminate our print materials (see order form). Also, **grant aid** to help cover our basic costs and to finance specific projects; and here we look to grant making trusts, to industry, to government, and also to individuals, perhaps through legacies.

The National Family Trust is a sign of hope. It needs your help now to sustain and extend its work.

change his child's surname. This is a question likely to arise if the mother forms a relationship with a new partner. Paternal grandparents may also be concerned about this. Giving a child a name is part of parental responsibility, and married parents may jointly name and rename their child. An unmarried father does not have parental responsibility unless he has acquired it by agreement with the mother or by court order. An unmarried mother who has sole parental responsibility, or a widow, may change her child's name to that of her new partner if she wants to. You can obtain advice about this by contacting:

- the Grandparents' Federation
- the Citizens Advice Bureau.

DISCOVERING GRANDPARENTS' RIGHTS

It seems odd to think that the **rights** of grandparents can be questioned. You are, as grandparents, entitled to think of yourselves as an extension of a family. No, more than that, you are *part* of that family.

However, sometimes a family is not without divisions. These can be caused by:

- divorce
- remarriage
- new partnerships
- moving away from the family.

Family quarrels, bitterness and jealousies can also divide families. You may find yourself separated from your grandchildren by any of these. If this happens you will need to enquire about your legal rights to see them. You should contact the following:

- a solicitor who is experienced in family/child law
- the Citizens Advice Bureau in your area
- the National Family Trust (see Figure 5)
- the Grandparents' Federation.

Being placed in care
Sadly it sometimes happens that children are placed in the care of the local authority. This may mean that they are fostered, or placed in a childrens' home. They might possibly be made wards of court.

It is reassuring to know (as mentioned in a previous chapter), that The Children Act was implemented in 1989. This means that you are now allowed to ask leave of court to apply for reasonable contact with your grandchildren. Again, you can get more information about the Act from the Grandparents' Federation.

Obtaining access to grandchildren

To be able to visit your family and see your grandchildren is something that all grandparents enjoy. If however, you are denied such access you are missing the important formative years in the development of your grandchildren. We have spoken of children being taken into care. Sometimes however, a parent will vanish, taking a child, or children with them.

There have been cases reported in the media, of children who are abducted and taken out of the country by either their natural father or mother. If you are in this situation it is wise to write to:

- your MP
- your Euro-MP if the child is to your knowledge, in an EU country.

If a child has been taken to a country that has implemented the European or Hague Convention on child abduction, then for information and help regarding the Hague Convention contact:

- The Lord Chancellor's Department.

Other agencies where you can obtain information are:

- Children's Legal Centre
- Reunite
- International Social Services.

Residence orders

You may want to settle arrangements about whether your grandchild or grandchildren live with you. This may mean applying for a residence order. Again, the Grandparents' Federation will advise you. You may however, be worried about costs involved in applying for the order, and the expenses you will incur by caring for grandchildren. Your solicitor or the Citizens Advice Bureau will advise you but there are also the following alternatives:

- If your local authority has been considering care proceedings but supports your application for a residence order, you may be eligible for help with legal costs.

- Find out from your local Benefits Agency office whether you are entitled to any financial help.

There may be times when you feel that the intensity and responsibility of being a grandparent is too much to bear. There are helplines available as Figure 6 illustrates, so use them.

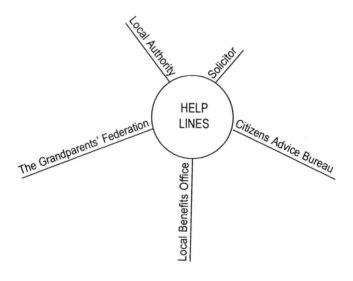

Fig. 6. Helplines available to grandparents.

CHECKLIST

- Suggest three things that would improve your relationship with your grandchildren.

- How often do you see your grandchildren?

- Make a list of where to go for help if you were denied access to your grandchildren.

CASE STUDIES

Joyce is a wise step-grandmother

Joyce is widowed and in her mid-sixties. Her only daughter Kate has two little girls and is separated from her husband. Joyce helped to look after her granddaughters when Kate was studying for a teaching degree.

It was during this time that Kate met Barry, who was a widower, much older than Kate. He had one daughter Lucy, a few years older than Joyce's granddaughters. Lucy was boisterous and ungainly, and completely different from the other two girls. Although able to accept Barry as her daughter's new partner, Joyce found it difficult to like her new step-grandchild. However, as all the children got on so well together, Joyce decided to try harder with Lucy. So, putting personal dislikes aside, she made a great effort and included all the grandchildren in anything she planned for them. She was careful not to comment on the differences she thought existed between the children.

This approach seemed to pay dividends, for when Lucy was older and went overseas to work, she wrote to Joyce, telling her how much she missed the treats that her step-grandmother had arranged for all of them. 'Although' she wrote, 'I must have been an awful shock for you to cope with!' This had of course, been true, but Joyce had very wisely put her own feelings aside and accepted Lucy as a welcome addition to the family.

Mary has a positive attitude

Mary is a widow in her fifties. Her children now all live away from home. Her youngest son Colin and his partner Sylvie live near her in a very small flat. When Sylvie became pregnant Mary was thrilled about becoming a grandmother for the first time, but she was concerned about the lack of space in the couple's flat. It was on the top floor of a block of similar flats, and the rooms were very cramped.

Mary's house is a large Victorian one, and with prior discussion with Colin and Sylvie, she went to see her bank manager. She was granted a loan, which was sufficient for a local builder to convert her house into two large flats. A reasonable rent was arranged and Mary took on two new roles of grandmother, and landlady. It was a positive approach to this situation, and even when the couple move out (they are saving to buy their own home), a tenant can always be found for the flat. This will help pay for the initial loan, and Mary will also have a source of income.

Mabel and Fred show restraint

Mabel and Fred are a couple in their early sixties. They have one married son who has a little girl, Sarah. Tragedy struck when Sarah started school. Their daughter-in law was diagnosed as having cancer, and died very soon after having a major operation.

After this, their son needed all their support, and particularly during the daytime, when they took Sarah to school and looked after her. Two years after his wife's death, their son met Ann, a divorcee with no children. Ann grew very fond of her newly acquired step-daughter. However, she was extremely jealous of the relationship Mabel and Fred had with the little girl. She refused to visit them, and only allowed them to see Sarah infrequently, and then not in her own home. She quarrelled with their son over his visits to his parents, and he was forced to limit these.

This distressing situation continued for several years. Mabel and Fred were mature enough to realise that at least they saw their granddaughter occasionally, and could keep in touch by telephoning their son. They did not apply for access rights, but did meet and discuss this with Ann and their son, who assured them that there was no need to enter into any such arrangements. The meeting served to show how deeply unhappy they were at not being able to see their granddaughter very often. They were restrained during this meeting, determined not to quarrel, which would have only made matters worse. They still do not see their granddaughter as often as they would like, but arrangements have been made for them to see her on a more regular basis.

DISCUSSION POINTS

1. Does being a step-grandparent bother you?

2. Do you have a favourite grandchild?

3. Do you keep in touch with your grandchildren?

4. Do you feel resentful in any way about being a grandparent?

5. Are you jealous when your grandchildren visit their other grandparents?

6. Are you able to talk over any problems that your grandchildren may have?

4
Being Supportive

Chapter 1 outlined some of the ways in which you can play a supporting role as a grandparent. This chapter looks in more detail at some of the practical and emotional ways in which you can give support. These include:

- helping financially
- assisting with sick or disabled children
- explaining problems
- being careful not to interfere.

HELPING WITH FINANCES

You may find that you are able to help out financially. This may mean that you advance a certain amount to your children to help pay for certain items that your grandchildren require. Today things are very expensive and items such as clothing, school equipment, sports outfits, musical instruments, books *etc*, may prove too much for a parent to cope with. If you are willing to give this kind of help do always remember to:

- discuss such arrangements with the parents
- decide what the most necessary items are
- settle on a certain amount and keep to this
- allow the parent (and grandchild if they are old enough) to choose their own personal items up to a fixed amount.

Giving a loan
A loan may prove helpful and you could put a time limit on when this should be repaid. It has been known of grandparents who have given a loan for some large item, for example a fridge or washing machine, only to find that the loan was not repaid. It is difficult to stipulate a time for repayment when lending money to relatives but

it is very important to make sure the arrangements are clear at the outset. Do try to make practical arrangements by:

- putting in writing the time limit of the loan
- suggesting weekly or monthly repayments that you know can be afforded.

Other ways to help financially

Your grandchild may be a full-time student and the education grant may not cover the extras your grandchild needs. You may be in a position to play a supportive role here. You would be wise however to explain how you intend to do this. Either go to see your grandchild (or the parents), or write stating how you feel that you can give financial support. Do remember to explain the following:

- The amounts you give are for a certain period only.

- The money you give is to be used in a particular way.

- You intend to give financial aid to all your grandchildren on an equal basis.

Investing large amounts

If you intend to invest a large amount in any of your grandchildren's future, *ie* education, business *etc*, then do consult the following:

- a financial adviser
- your bank manager
- the Citizens Advice Bureau.

Making a will

For your own peace of mind, do not forget to make your will. It is an important item, but one that may be overlooked. You may merely need to update your current will, or you may never have had time to actually have a will drawn up. It is always wise to put in writing how you would like your money, and indeed other things to be distributed after your death. Figure 7 illustrates the consequences of *not* making a will, so it is always advisable to do so. It is in such a document that you can actually specify a child's name (or childrens' names), or indeed any other relatives' names that you would like to be known as your beneficiaries.

Some Citizens Advice Bureaux actually assist in the drawing up of a will. Alternatively your solicitor will advise you.

In whatever way you decide to give financial help, your support in this way, will prove very helpful. However, always be diplomatic in how you approach this matter.

ASSISTING WITH SICK OR DISABLED CHILDREN

When children are sick or handicapped the pressures on parents can be great, especially when there are other children to look after. Grandparents can be particularly supportive either during a temporary childhood illness or when there is a child who needs more full-time care.

Giving support when a grandchild is ill

The illness may be of a long duration, with perhaps, frequent hospital attendance and treatment. It is obviously easier if you live near your grandchild, and are able to visit him or her in hospital. Visits to cheer your grandchild however, can be arranged even if you are not in the locality. It is not only that your grandchild needs to be visited, but it is important to show the parents that you are willing to be supportive.

If the child is ill at home, again you can visit, perhaps helping in

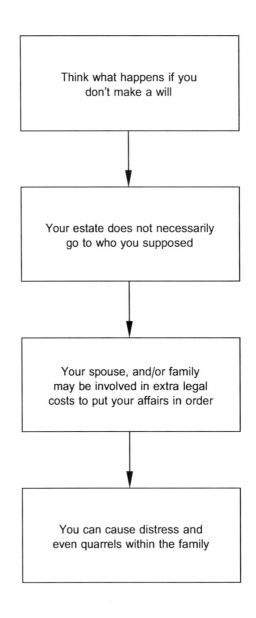

Fig. 7. The consequences of not making a will.

the home in some way, or minding other members of the family. Just feeding the cats and taking dogs for a walk are all small items, but time consuming. It will be a relief for the parent or parents if it is possible for you to take on these jobs. Just by visiting when possible, or by offering your help in practical ways the family will know you are supportive.

The premature birth of a baby can give rise to a great deal of anxiety for the parents. Your help and support will be valued if your grandchild is born prematurely, particularly if there are other children in the family who will need minding during the parents' frequent visits to the hospital. Action Research, a charity dedicated to preventing and treating disease and disability by funding vital medical research, has produced a practical guide for parents of babies born prematurely, called *Born Too Early*. This guide is designed to answer clearly and simply the questions that parents will have concerning their baby. Details of how to obtain a copy are in the further reading section at the end of this book.

Helping when a grandchild is disabled

You may be asked for help, or you may be concerned if you have a grandchild who is disabled in some way. This may be due to a condition that has existed from birth, or may have arisen through illness or accident later on. It is important to know where you can go to get help and advice.

Most doctors will have details of other organisations where you can obtain more specialised help. The Citizens Advice Bureau will also be able to help you with various contacts and your local Social Services may also be able to help you. For their address and telephone number, look under your local County or Borough Council's name in the telephone book and the subheading Social Services. When you telephone ask to speak to the Social Services department for the city, town or village in which your grandchild resides. Explain that you wish to speak to someone in relation to what assistance is available for children with disabilities.

Disability and financial assistance

If you have a grandchild who is disabled, you may be worried that this is an added financial burden on the parent, or parents. Travelling to and from hospital for specialised treatment for example, can be expensive.

For general advice regarding Social Security Benefits for disabled people a Freephone service is available (0800 88 22 00).

- Benefit enquiry line (address and telephone number are given at the back of this book).

For advice about social security benefits you can telephone the following:

- Disability rights advice line. (The Disability Alliance Educational Research Association.) Address and telephone number at the back of this book.

Contacting helpful organisations

There are many local and national self-help groups and organisations that can offer advice and help. They vary with regard to what they offer. Some offer practical support and others provide help and support through family centres, as well as daycare centres, community and neighbourhood centres. One organisation provides a nationwide team of professional social workers who visit families with a physically disabled child, and giving practical and sometimes financial support to children with arthritic conditions and limb deficiencies. Another organisation supports UK-wide disability information and advice services.

Organisations that offer such support, include:

- **The Lady Hoare Trust for Physically Disabled Children** (help for children with arthritis or limb disabilities).

- **The Children's Society** (registered as Church of England Children's Society). One of Britain's oldest charities, works with some of the nation's most vulnerable children, who face poverty, abuse, as well as homelessness and exploitation. Listens to children, and encourages planners, policy-makers and educators to do the same. Offers practical advice to families about budgeting and debt management. Encourages self-help groups. Offers help in the home, support and advice to families who have a child with a disability.

- **RADAR (The Royal Association for Disability and Rehabilitation)**. A national organisation working with and for disabled people. Offers information and advice on all issues relating to disability. Produces a wide range of publications and fact-packs, supports over 500 member groups. Believes that where possible, disabled children and students should receive education alongside their peers.

- **The Disability Law Service**. This service gives free legal advice and representation to disabled people and/or carers throughout Britain.

- **DIAL (Disability Information and Advice Lines)** is an organisation that covers many things relevant to those who have any disability. It supports UK-wide disability information and advice services. (See your local telephone directory for local branches.)

- **The Snowdon Award Scheme** was founded in 1981 by the Earl of Snowdon in order to assist physically disabled young people entering further education.

Organisations for the blind and deaf
There are a number of organisations specifically for the blind and the deaf but probably the most widely known are:

- **Royal National Institute for Deaf People (RNID)**. There is a local information service via regional offices (list available).

- **Royal National Institute for the Blind.**

- **The National Deafblind and Rubella Association (SENSE).**

- **Action for Blind People**. Deals with many things including information and advice on employment, grants and benefits.

- **The National Deaf Children's Society**. This Society has a freephone helpline which is open from Monday – Friday, 1p.m. – 5p.m.

Addresses and telephone numbers for all the organisations listed here can be found at the end of this book.

EXPLAINING PROBLEMS

If your family experiences problems involving your grandchild one way you could show your support is by offering to contact, on their behalf, any of the relevant organisations which may be able to help or give advice. Some of these organisations have already been listed and there are still others at the end of the book in the useful addresses section. Explaining a problem to someone trained to deal specifically with such matters can, if nothing else, help to put things in perspective.

Contacting advisers

When you find the name of an organisation or person who you think may be able to help, telephone or write to them. Mention the following points:

1. Explain that you are speaking on behalf of your grandchild and family.

2. Ask if you can make an appointment to discuss the particular problem you are concerned about.

3. State briefly what the problem is.

4. If you feel that the problem is one that is too personal or confidential to discuss over the telephone, then explain this and say that you would prefer to call in to discuss it.

5. If this organisation or person cannot help you, then ask if they can suggest another organisation you can contact.

Explaining problems to other members of the family

Grandchildren can sometimes bring problems to you that you feel should be discussed with the parents. By all means do this, but be careful to tackle this by:

1. Explaining to your grandchild that this problem needs to be discussed more fully with his or her parents.

2. Remaining calm and trying to avoid a scene.

3. Getting all the correct facts together that relate to this problem.

4. Pointing out how much this problem is affecting your grandchild.

Explaining problems to the authorities

Sometimes certain problems arise that may mean involving certain authorities. Perhaps the police are called upon, or a doctor or solicitor are required. When you speak to them explain that:

• You are acting in your grandchild's interests.

• You have certain facts that might prove helpful.

- You are willing to assist the authorities.

- You want to remain in contact with your grandchild (or grandchildren).

It may be difficult for you in some instances to try and resolve or get help over problems, but it is important that difficulties are overcome to ensure the happiness of your grandchildren. Whoever you contact to solve a problem, explaining it to someone objective will help in a number of ways.

AVOIDING INTERFERING

You would be surprised and hurt if you overheard yourself being described as an 'interfering' grandparent. As a grandparent it is important to know the difference between giving support or taking an interest and **interfering**.

A case study

Lydia always had an excellent relationship with her daughter and her grandchildren who were now in their teens. She lived in the same town and although widowed, she had a number of friends and enjoyed her independence. Perhaps she was over-confident in her relationship with the grandchildren, but one day while she was visiting her daughter, she overheard her eldest granddaughter saying to the youngest, 'Oh, don't let Gran upset you, she doesn't like any of our friends, you know what she says about them.'

On her way home, Lydia kept thinking of all the things she'd said in the past about the friends that her grandchildren brought home. Yes, she could remember making comments like, 'you're not still going out with Greg are you? He's so arrogant.' Quite ordinary comments, she'd thought at the time, but she realised now, that although she'd been tolerated because she was 'Gran', her words had offended and she had been labelled as 'interfering'.

Avoiding the same mistakes

It is wise to be careful before making such comments, so try to avoid the following:

- making personal comments about any of your grandchildren's friends

- passing judgement on your grandchildren, their friends, clothes, hobbies *etc.*

Being diplomatic

Whether you are giving **financial**, **practical**, or **emotional** support it is always important to be **diplomatic** in your approach.

Financially

Be careful not to discuss how you are helping your grandchildren financially with any of their friends or other relatives. The fact that you are favouring certain members of the family may provoke resentment or jealousy. It is advisable to consult the parents before offering financial help to a grandchild before they, for example, go away to university. Try to find out which would be the best way you could provide financial help.

Practical help

As a grandparent you will most likely have helped, or be prepared to help in a practical way. However, when visiting your grandchildren do not start clearing up, what you consider to be a mess they may have made in the living room or elsewhere.

They may have left magazines, books, tapes, videos *etc* scattered about, but it is *their* house, and *their* things. It is all too easy to assume that your help is required, but this may at some time look like interference on your part. Unless you are asked, or have made sure that you are helping:

Don't throw away anything that looks like rubbish. Always check to find out if anything is still needed.

Don't enter their room to tidy up.

Being loving

On occasions your grandchildren, or a grandchild may quarrel with their parents, particularly during the teenage years when moods fluctuate. You may be the person to whom a grandchild will turn, and pour out some grievance. This, however, is a difficult position to be in, especially if that grievance is directed against another member of the family. You will want to respond lovingly, and this is natural. However, be careful not to take sides. You can provoke a quarrel this way, especially if any of your words are repeated. You do not want to antagonise any member of the family, so it is best to:

- Calm your grandchild down.

- Listen carefully to what he or she has to say.

- Find out if the problem is serious and use your judgement about what you should do and who you should approach about the matter.

Show by your attitude, how concerned you are for your grandchild. If you have a good relationship with this child, or any of your grandchildren, they will know without question, not only that you love them and will support them, but that you must also be fair to others in the family.

QUESTIONS AND ANSWERS

I want to leave my property and my money to my grandchildren as well as my children. Who can advise me about this?

If you have a solicitor do consult him or her about this. If you need the name of a solicitor who can help you, contact the Citizens Advice Bureau.

Our grandson is partially disabled through crippling arthritis. Is there an organisation that the family can contact for advice and support?

Yes, The Lady Hoare Trust for Physically Disabled Children offers such help for children with arthritis or limb problems.

My only granddaughter is a student and badly needs extra financial help. Would I be wise to make arrangements to give her a monthly allowance?

Before you do this, check with your granddaughter's parents to ensure that they know what you intend, and that they do not object to this. Once you have their consent then make the necessary arrangements.

CHECKLIST

- List three ways in which you could assist your grandchild financially.

- List three organisations you could contact if you needed advice regarding a disabled child.

- What would you do if your grandchild quarrelled with her parents and came to you for help? How would you make sure you were diplomatic?

CASE STUDIES

Maureen worries about interfering

Maureen is a widow in her early sixties. Her only daughter Katrina is divorced and lives with her 12-year-old daughter Joanne, and her new partner Brian.

Maureen had always been supportive throughout her daughter's traumatic marriage and divorce, but she is reluctant to interfere in Katrina's new life with Brian. She was pleased when they met and when Brian moved in with Katrina and her granddaughter. He is a hardworking man and keen to be a good stepfather to Joanne. However, Joanne is causing problems. She is antagonistic towards Brian, and is jealous of his relationship with her mother. She remains loyal to her father. Now approaching her early teens, she is sulky both with Brian and her mother.

Maureen worries about the situation, but is concerned that any help she gives to her granddaughter may appear to be interfering.

Joanne, however, has always been very fond of her 'Nan'. Before Brian moved in with them she used to spend the occasional night at Maureen's home. Now she won't leave her mother alone in the house with Brian. Maureen thinks she would be able to talk to Joanne if she stayed with her for a while, over a weekend, or during the school holidays perhaps.

When she suggested this to Katrina and Brian however, they were hurt, as they felt this implied that they could not cope with Joanne. 'I didn't mean to interfere,' Maureen assured them. She explained that a short while away from her own home, in a different environment, might help Joanne to come to terms with the changes that had taken place in her young life. Fortunately, Maureen had always had a good relationship with her daughter, or they might have quarrelled. Katrina explained to her mother how she and Brian felt about the suggestion she'd made: 'It might look to Joanne as though we are excluding her from family life with us, which is the last thing she needs right now.'

Maureen had to agree. They finally worked out a compromise,

and it was decided that Maureen could take Joanne out on extra trips, *eg* to the cinema *etc*. She also convinced Joanne that she needed help to take up swimming again.

Joanne enjoys sport, and this suited her, particularly as she felt she was helping her Nan. These trips began to relax Joanne and she eventually became confident enough to spend the occasional night at Maureen's house again.

Obviously her feelings towards Brian will fluctuate, and coming to terms with her emotions will take time. She is less defiant in her attitude towards him now however, and things do hopefully, seem set to improve.

Finding a helpful organisation

Hilda and Edward who are in their seventies, have several grandchildren. One of them is Jason, a nine-year-old. Jason suffers from juvenile chronic arthritis and is disabled. He and his parents live in a rural area, and Hilda and Edward are concerned because the treatment centre which Jason attends is several miles away and the journey is costly. They feel too, that the family may be isolated, and that the extra costs of certain things like the extra heating needed to ensure that their grandchild is kept warm is proving to be a considerable worry to the family. They are trying to find ways to help ease these worries, and looking for any organisations that can assist them.

Hilda and Edward called on their local Citizens Advice Bureau and explained how concerned they were about Jason and his family. They were told about several organisations which help disabled people. One of these, The Lady Hoare Trust for Physically Disabled Children is committed to helping children up to the age of 18 who are disabled by arthritis, as well as limb disabilities.

Hilda and Edward offered to contact this organisation on behalf of Jason's parents. When they did they discovered that a great deal of support was available. They were able to tell Jason's parents, that the Trust runs a network of social workers throughout the UK who regularly visit, support and counsel families. The Trust can assist sometimes with small grants to help cover the extra costs involved with caring for a child with a disability.

The whole family was reassured. Hilda and Edward were also relieved when they heard that the Trust is able to act as the family's representative with other professional bodies, and will help to put families in touch with others in similar situations. They knew now that the family would not be isolated any longer.

Financial help wisely tackled

Jan and Ian had worked hard all their lives and invested savings wisely. So now, in their retirement they have capital with which to enjoy a good quality of life.

They had, several times, given money to Jeremy their only grandson when he had got into debt as a university student. He has now finished his university course, and has found a satisfactory job. They want to help him financially at the start of his career, but do not want him to use the money unwisely. They decided to arrange a meeting with Jeremy and be very frank with him. At the meeting they suggested a way to help him but they also stipulated that some of the money should be repaid at some future date.

Jeremy told his grandparents that he had rented a small flat not far from his place of employment. They decided that if they loaned him anything that he would repay them in two years' time. After some discussion they all agreed that an agreement could be drawn up whereby Jan and Ian paid the first six months' rent on the flat, and that Jeremy repaid half the amount in two years' time.

'This will replace some of the capital we use,' Ian explained. The amount loaned to Jeremy would enable him to furnish the flat, something that at present he could ill afford to do. All of them were happy about the arrangements they had made.

Amy helps when her grandchild is born prematurely

Amy is 59 and her only daughter Ruth is married and pregnant. This is after years of trying to have a baby and naturally, everyone is overjoyed.

Ruth has been in reasonable health during the pregnancy and it came as a shock when the baby was born prematurely. She was concerned about how she would cope when she brought the baby home from the hospital. Amy who knew very little about premature births, was also concerned. She set out to help her daughter, and was relieved to find that there are organisations that are able to give advice.

Amy practically moved into her daughter's house, when the new baby was allowed to leave hospital. She took over the cooking, and saw to the washing *etc*. In fact, she kept the routine in the house running smoothly. She also telephoned the Citizens Advice Bureau, and asked if they could give her the name of any organisation that could give advice about babies born prematurely.

The Citizens Advice Bureau gave Amy the name of Action Research who recommended their guide for parents of babies born prematurely called *Born Too Early*.

The baby continued to thrive, and Amy was gradually able to leave her daughter in control again. She was, her daughter knew, always willing to help whenever necessary.

DISCUSSION POINTS

1. If a grandchild complained to you about a parent would you find this difficult to cope with?

2. Would it be possible for you to act in a supportive role if a grandchild were ill?

3. How would you offer assistance to the family with a sick or disabled child?

" BEING SUPPORTIVE "

5
Coping with Divided Families

Following a separation or divorce there may be a division of family loyalties and it is of course, very difficult not to take sides. Sometimes family relationships have been known to break down completely with children losing contact with a parent or grandparents, which causes grief for all those involved. Pages 13 and 14 in Chapter 1 offer some advice about where grandparents should turn if they are denied access to their grandchildren. This chapter however, deals with:

- how you can support your grandchildren in the initial stages of a relationship breaking down
- trying to be fair to all concerned
- coming to terms with a new family structure
- treating grandchildren and step-grandchildren equally.

KEEPING CALM

If a separation or divorce takes place between the parents of your grandchildren try to remain calm. Although it is natural for you to be upset, the most important people at this time will be your grandchildren who will need your reassurance, love and support. You can support them through this difficult time in a number of ways:

1. By bringing a sense of order into their disrupted lives.

2. By helping children to hang on to their self-esteem – they may feel it is they who are at fault in some way.

3. By making sure they know they are still loved.

During a period of unhappy marriage or partnership, the underlying problems are not always revealed until divorce or separation proceedings are underway. Depending on the ages of the children involved in this sort of break-up, their reasoning about the problems involved will be bound up with the fact that they are facing the loss of someone they love, or who they have come to know well. By maintaining contact, and staying calm during the stressful period of a family break-up, you will be a supportive grandparent who your grandchildren will know they can turn to in the future.

TRYING TO BE FAIR

Nowadays the terms ex-husband/wife or ex-son/daughter-in-law are heard all too often. Grandparents should try to avoid using the prefix 'ex', particularly in front of the children.

If for any reason you are caught up in an argument between the separating couple try and be fair and listen to all sides. It is especially important that your grandchildren perceive you as being fair to both their parents.

Ultimately however, you have to try to accept that the relationship between two people you are fond of may be over. Concentrate now, on being there for the grandchildren. If you can't always be there physically make sure you stay in touch by speaking to them regularly on the telephone. Keep the conversation light and don't allow any bitterness you may feel to come over to them. Always show an interest in what they are doing such as hobbies, sports *etc*, and plan your next visit to them or vice versa so they have something to look forward to.

As time goes on your grandchildren will become fully aware that you are coping with the same situation they are. But for now, by remaining calm, treating all members of the family fairly and trying to dispel any bitterness, you will provide some stability and support during this bewildering and stressful time.

Understanding children's reactions

Each child will respond differently to the breakdown of the parental relationship. One child will cry, another may display anger over what appear to be minor things, another may stop working at school and yet another may become withdrawn. You may need to seek help yourself in order to understand how you should deal with the different reactions displayed by your grandchildren. Either approach your doctor yourself or suggest to a parent that the child would benefit from a consultation with the family doctor.

Contact the National Council for One-Parent Families to obtain a copy of their book *How to Help* which is produced to help the family and friends of lone parents. See the useful addresses section at the end of this book.

COMING TO TERMS WITH A NEW FAMILY

How would you react if you had to come to terms with a **new family**? The family you have known, maybe for a long time, has changed. Sadly, in some cases, this change may be caused by the death of one of the parents of your grandchildren. Perhaps the partner who is left is planning to remarry. You and your grandchildren will hopefully, have helped each other through the period of grief which you've all shared. Now the children are going to have a new parent in their home so be supportive, and use tact and understanding at all times.

Acquiring a new family

You may find you become step-grandparents if:

1. Your own child marries someone who already has children by a previous marriage.

2. You are widowed or divorced and marry someone who has their own grandchildren.

Would you find this new situation easy to cope with? You might be a little apprehensive but remember your new grandchildren will be just as apprehensive. It will help if you try and remember the following:

(a) Don't compare your new grandchildren with those you have known for a long time.
(b) Assure the parents that you wish to help.
(c) Ignore any resentful attitudes that children may show.

Extending a welcome to the new members of the family can be made more difficult if one of the parents does not have custody of their own children.

Example

Joan was not allowed contact with her granddaughter for some years. It was difficult for her to accept her new stepgrandson as part of her family. She began to realise however, that the situation was just as hard for her son who missed his daughter, now that she lived with his ex-wife. 'It is a confusing situation for three generations to be in,' Joan confided to her friend, 'one in which anxiety, as well as bitterness are entwined.'

New family problems
Sometimes, although you may be making every effort to make your new grandchildren feel welcome they may also feel resentful about being part of a new family. A small child may not wish to call you 'Grannie', or 'Grandpa'. Older children and teenagers may show positive hostility against you as new grandparents. Time, and your patience, are the only things you have to work with.

1. Don't let yourself be hurt by a child's attitude.

2. Try not to show annoyance or even anger if you are upset by a child's remarks.

3. Try not to resent your new step-grandchildren if you are unable to see your own grandchildren.

4. Don't interfere with new family arrangements.

One organisation that works towards increasing public awareness and acceptance of the stepfamily is known as 'Stepfamily'. This organisation offers a helpline service (see Figure 8). Their address is to be found at the back of this book.

Variations on grandparenting today
Times may have changed, but your role as a grandparent has not. Family life may differ from what you have known. For instance:

(a) You may be a grandparent to a child who has more than one other adult figure assuming parental responsibility in their life.

(b) You may be sharing the enjoyment of your grandchildren and step-grandchildren, with other grandparents.

(c) You may have grandchildren who have become part of a family which may now include other children who are not of the same parents, and who may even have a different culture.

FAMILY PUZZLES ???

Should I discipline my stepchildren?

I love my kids more than his, am I wrong?

How can I be friends with my husband's children?

Now we've got our own baby she wants me to see less of my kids, what should I do?

How do I see my grandchildren now that my daughter-in-law has remarried?

Why should I have to pay for my stepson to loaf around all day?

What shall we do at Christmas?

Should I change my family rules when his kids come to visit?

How do I tell my stepdaughter to wear more clothes around the house?

How can I tell my son his father is really his stepfather?

Will a child of our own bring us all closer?

Rover and Tiddles | Peter's stepson | Anne's dad | Sue's ex-husband's mum

Anne's mum's boyfriend | Their new baby | Jamie's new sister | John's dad's girlfriend

How hard do I have to try?

When is there time for us?

I'm not sure if I'm a stepfamily but...

0990 168 388

STEPFAMILY
Challenging the Myths

Helpline Monday to Friday 2-5 or 7-10pm

What do I call my mum's boyfriend or my dad's girlfriend?

Will they love their new baby more than me?

Do I have to do what my stepdad says?

I'm not the eldest any more, why can't things stay the way they were?

How do I tell my stepfather to wear more clothes around the house?

Can I go and live with my dad?

Can I change my name to yours?

I want my Dad to give me away but I don't want to upset my Mum, what shall I do?

If you or your partner have children from a previous partnership then you are a stepfamily.
That means your parents could be step-grandparents!
Over two million children are growing up as part of a stepfamily.

Fig. 8. 'Stepfamily' offers a helpline service.

Ideally you will want to be gently supportive grandparents. This may not be as easy to accomplish as you think, but it is possible to achieve. There are now many types of families, more loosely knit than ever. The stability that grandparents can bring to the family, is, as always, important. Love, patience, tolerance, and diplomacy are the vital ingredients necessary to ensure a good and permanent relationship within the family structure.

TREATING GRANDCHILDREN AND STEP-GRANDCHILDREN EQUALLY

Treating your step-grandchildren like your own isn't as easy as it might sound – there won't be the same bond between you and the step-grandchildren. You might also feel some prejudice against your son or daughter's new partner which will inevitably cloud your judgement of their children. Consequently you may not be as fair or impartial as you would like to be.

It will help you to develop a relationship with your step-grandchildren if you find mutual interests to discuss. You will have to try to be very patient and perhaps accept that you may be onlookers, and not such active members of this new family for a little while, until everyone starts to feel a little more secure.

Explaining and sharing

Sometimes, the **sharing** of their grandparents, may be very distressing for children. You may be aware of the jealousy existing between your own grandchildren and their stepbrothers or stepsisters. If you are able to see all your grandchildren (including step-grandchildren) often, then you may feel it necessary or helpful to discuss this with them. There are ways to do this depending on the age of the children:

(a) Explain that although the changes in family life are difficult to accept, you are trying to come to terms with them yourself.

(b) Make it plain that you are there to support, love and encourage them.

(c) Demonstrate your love with younger children. Give those all important hugs. Try not to exclude your step-grandchildren from this token of affection.

(d) Use your common sense with regard to not provoking jealousy amongst the children in the family.

Do not rush things, give yourself, your grandchildren, and your step-grandchildren time to adjust.

QUESTIONS AND ANSWERS

My son is now divorced from a girl that both my husband and I had come to like very much. He is now living with someone else, and appears to be very happy. We are finding it very difficult to accept that she has taken the place of our daughter-in-law. How can we cope with this situation?

This problem is difficult, but not insurmountable. First of all, remember that your son is happy. His new partner may be feeling strange with you and your husband as 'step-family'. Try to behave as naturally as possible when you see her. Make a point of discussing only what is relevant to the present, never (unless the matter is first broached by her, or your son) dwell on the past, or his ex-wife. What you are feeling is a sort of grief for the person you knew and liked. In time this grief will ease, and at the moment it is important for you not to compare your son's new partner with his ex-wife.

My youngest daughter has been left alone by the father of their year old child. She feels very isolated, and does not live nearby. Is there some organisation that I could tell her about that could advise and guide her through this rather difficult time?

Obviously you can be supportive from a distance, because being able to talk to you is vital. You could tell her of the National Council for One Parent Families (address at the back of this book). This association supplies helpful information to lone parents about support groups and services available in their area.

Our son who was widowed quite young has now remarried. He has two teenage sons, and they have settled in quite happily with their new step-mum and her son of ten. He is quieter than the other two, and seems rather shy. We want to show him that he is included in all we do. How should we set about this?

Find out what he is interested in so that you are able to discuss these things with him. Be patient, he may well be shy, or simply quietly finding out how he fits into this new relationship. Encourage him to join in all the activities that you and the others share. If he has other grandparents let him talk about them if he wants to. It may be confusing for him to accept that he has you also now. Let him see that you care for him just as you do the others.

CHECKLIST

- List the ways that you can keep in touch with your grandchildren if they live a long way from you.

- List the ways in which you could help bring back stability to your family's life.

- If you found it difficult to cope with new step-grandchildren what organisation could prove helpful?

CASE STUDIES

Gwen learns from her mistake

Gwen Rysdale is a 70-year-old widowed grandmother. She lives in Lincolnshire and has brought up three children. Her daughter Lisa is now the only one of her children who lives near her.

Gwen is resourceful and lively but she is known for her quick temper. As one of her sons says: 'She doesn't pull any punches!'

Gwen paid dearly for commenting on the way that her new son-in-law was bringing up Kylie, her six-year-old granddaughter. Her daughter is divorced from Kylie's father, and has remarried Ben. Gwen had been fond of Kylie's dad, and disappointed when her daughter's relationship with him had ended.

She had been quick to notice any small differences in how her daughter's new husband treated Kylie. Her daughter had asked her not to interfere on more than one occasion when Gwen had angrily accused Ben of being too sharp with her granddaughter. It was when Ben decided to take Kylie away from the local village school (which all Gwen's children had attended), and send her to another some distance away that Gwen quarrelled with him. This quarrel had split the family. A lot of resentments that Gwen had been harbouring, about Ben's attitude in general, came into the quarrel. Later, Ben told her daughter that her mother was overbearing and biased against him. He refused to visit Gwen, or to allow her in his home. He also told his wife that she was not to let Gwen see Kylie.

Gwen was devastated. Denied access to both her daughter and her granddaughter, she eventually wrote to Ben asking him to meet her 'on neutral ground'. Fortunately, he agreed (possibly persuaded by Gwen's daughter). Gwen apologised, admitting that she should not have interfered. She and Ben reached a truce of sorts, and she now visits her daughter and sees Kylie again at regular intervals.

Sylvia resolves the problems with her step-grandchildren

Sylvia aged 64 is widowed, with a daughter and granddaughter who live abroad. She met and married Ronald quickly. Ronald is a widower in his late sixties. He owns a travel agency and is comfortably off. He has a son who is married, with one daughter, and also a married daughter who has two sons. They all live locally, and although they seemed to like Sylvia when they first met her, they demanded a lot of Ronald's time and frequently asked him for money. He never refused them anything. When he treated them to shows and holidays he did not include Sylvia, and she began to feel isolated.

For several months Sylvia tried to come to terms with the demands her step-children, and step-grandchildren made on Ronald's time and money. When she tried to discuss it with Ronald he accused her of being jealous of his family.

'It's just that you never do anything without asking them about it', she argued. Ronald told the family about their argument, which made matters worse. She had hoped to be able to enjoy the company of her step-grandchildren, as her own family was abroad. However, the new grandchildren sided with their parents and grandfather, and Sylvia felt alone and helpless. She didn't know how to cope with the situation.

A friend told her about The National Stepfamily Association, who has a helpline which is open for six hours each week and is run by qualified counsellors. She received excellent help and advice and after a while she persuaded Ronald to join the association too. Eventually he was able to understand the difficulties she was experiencing. Although certain things will remain the same, he now makes much more effort to include Sylvia in more things. She now feels happier about her marriage, and her relationship with the other members of the family has improved.

DISCUSSION POINTS

1. Do you find it difficult to be friendly with your step-

grandchildren if you are not allowed contact with your own grandchildren?

2. If your grandchild was obviously emotionally disturbed because his parents had separated where would you go for help?

3. How difficult is it for you not to intervene in a family quarrel?

4. What would be your reaction if a step-grandchild resented you?

5. Where do you feel that your responsibility as a grandparent ends?

" DIVIDED FAMILIES"

6
Entertaining Grandchildren

Entertaining and organising the family and the grandchildren can take a great deal of your time and most of your energy. This chapter discusses:

- the need to plan a daily routine if you are minding your grandchildren
- arranging holidays
- planning how to entertain your grandchildren when they visit
- organising family occasions.

PLANNING A DAILY ROUTINE

As a grandparent you may be helping out by looking after your grandchildren for certain times of the day on a regular basis. This may be during:

- school holidays
- when a parent is ill
- a period of stress when parents are unable to cope with a child (or children)
- while a parent is at work.

For whatever reason you are minding a child it is best to have some sort of routine. This is particularly necessary if you are intending to have your grandchild on a regular basis.

Having a routine is not only practical, it is also reassuring for children to know what is going to happen each day. In this way their day has a familiar pattern which helps to bring a sense of stability into their lives. Let's plan an imaginary day. Perhaps you have a grandchild during the day, one who is too young to attend school, and not yet established at a nursery school. The following plan may be helpful:

1. Collect your grandchild or if he is brought to the house make sure you greet him enthusiastically.

2. Encourage your grandchild to take off his own coat *etc* and put them in the same place each day.

3. Begin your day together by either having a chat about what he did the day before or perhaps by reading a story.

4. Keep a box of toys, *etc* in the same place for him to get out and enjoy.

5. Have a break for a drink and perhaps a snack – this could coincide with a favourite morning children's television programme, which you could enjoy together.

6. Plan some sort of craft session. Either drawing or colouring (or painting if you're brave enough!) for him to do whilst you are close at hand or perhaps do some cooking, or cutting and pasting together.

7. Plan to have lunch at approximately the same time each day.

8. After lunch is a good time to have a rest (both of you) either your grandchild may like to have a sleep or just sit down together and enjoy a quiet story.

9. Depending on the weather try and get outside for a walk and some fresh air during the afternoon – a stroll to the park to feed the ducks. Rainy day activities could include outings to the local swimming pool.

10. Home for tea and preparation for going home.

A sense of order is very important in a child's day. This is particularly necessary if they have a parent who is ill, away, or in hospital. Order in their young lives helps provide reassurance.

Looking after older grandchildren

The grandchildren you have been asked to look after could be of school age in which case they may come to you after school to wait for a parent to take them home. If this is the case try to remember the following:

- Always be on time if you have to collect them from school.

- Make sure you are always at home waiting if they walk to your house from school.

- Be ready to listen if they want to talk.

- Have a snack and drink ready for them when they get in or make sure they know where to find it for themselves.

- Allow them time to relax without continually asking them about their day. They may want to flop in front of the television for a while and 'switch off'.

- If possible give them their own space in your home, so that they can get on with some homework if they need to.

Be prepared for after school 'moods' which may have been triggered by a quarrel with a friend at school. Stay calm but be firm:

1. Avoid an argument over something trivial.

2. Allow them time to unwind if they appear upset about something.

3. Act normally.

4. If a grandchild is rude try not to get angry but explain that this is not what you expect from them.

5. Try and maintain a sense of humour – it can sometimes help to defuse a 'mood'.

ARRANGING HOLIDAYS

Holidays can be lots of fun but they can also be fraught, as we all know. Sunburn, rain, tired children and exhausted parents and grandparents are familiar to us all. However, although the weather can never be predicted, careful arrangements about holidays can prove beneficial.

Having the family to stay
If the whole family comes to stay with you, have some meals out.

This can be in the form of a picnic, a pub lunch, or something else, but will save on your energy and you will be less tired at the end of the day. Planning in this way helps you to enjoy the holiday too. Try not to be concerned if:

- The house becomes very untidy.

- The children quarrel amongst themselves.

- The weather is dreadful (you can do nothing about this, except have indoor games, books, and comics ready).

- You find the children are allowed to eat more sweets, and watch more TV than you think is good for them. If their parents are with them, this is their responsibility.

Plan menus in advance. Find out what foods they like and dislike. Sometimes, older children like to take turns in cooking. A barbeque with dad, or granddad in charge can be great fun. Remember to use plastic plates, as well as throw-away cups when eating outside. If the weather is fine, think of the amount of washing-up that will be avoided.

Going away with the family
If you are going camping, or staying in a cottage or hotel think about how everyone is going to entertain themselves if the weather is bad.

- Find out beforehand, if possible, if there are any local entertainments, *eg* leisure centre or cinema.

- Contact the local tourist information office to find out what places of interest you could visit.

- Take cagoules and wellingtons for walking in bad weather.

- Take a supply of books, jigsaws, paper, paints, and a compendium of games. Older children will be sure to take their personal stereos as well as books and videos.

If there are several adults in the party, make a rota for planning menus, shopping, arranging outings *etc*. There will certainly be some heated discussion about some of these things.

ORGANISING YOUR GRANDCHILDRENS' VISITS

You may be planning to have your grandchildren to stay with you during their holidays and the prospect of this is always pleasant. However, remember that children get bored, so have some idea before they arrive about how you are going to entertain them.

1. Outline a plan for each day that they are with you. Make it flexible though to accommodate the weather, *ie* a cinema trip when it rains.

2. Find out what sort of things the children like to do and if there is anywhere specific they would like to go.

3. If a long car ride is planned, keep the children occupied with *eg* games of I-Spy. Older children will probably want to take their personal stereos. Consider borrowing story tapes from the local library.

4. As well as snacks and drinks for the car, don't forget the first-aid box.

Having younger grandchildren to stay
If young children are staying with you without their parents, remember that they are likely to get homesick at times. Make sure that they bring something with them that is very familiar – a favourite toy or teddy. Some children enjoy the feel of a certain piece of cloth – whatever the comforter is, have it ready – especially at night.

Having older children to stay
If your grandchildren are older and you live near a large city, they may want to go about on their own and use your home as a base. You could suggest that you accompany them sometimes, but try not to be offended if they don't seem enthusiastic about this – young people like their independence. To be helpful you could:

1. Have a bus timetable in your home for your grandchildren to refer to.

2. Be willing to drive them to the bus or train or the venue of their choice.

3. Find out the opening and closing times of museums, shops and galleries *etc.*

4. Discuss and decide on a time by which they should be home at night.

Showing them around the area

Your home may be near the sea, or in the country and this may be part of the enjoyment for grandchildren when they visit you. You may want to show them around the area so if they are older children, ask if you can:

1. Take them out to visit a certain place that you know they will like.

2. Offer to transport them to the beach. It may be that you would like a day at the sea as well.

3. If their parents are with them, organise plans for each day, including menus and shopping.

Make sure that you too, enjoy the holiday.

ORGANISING FAMILY OCCASIONS

Organising family get-togethers involve someone having to spend a great deal of time, effort and often money making the arrangements.

Organising a party

Perhaps one of your grandchildren is getting engaged, or someone has a special birthday or anniversary all of which can be occasions for a family party. First of all, however, make sure the person or couple involved actually want a party and then start to plan.

1. How much will the party cost?

2. Will it be necessary to hire a hall or is it possible to hold the party at home?

3. Who is to be invited?

Keep a record of how much is spent on the following:

- the caterers
- food
- drink
- hire of hall
- other items *eg* flowers.

Check the dates that halls are available before you finalise the date of the party – they do tend to get booked up very quickly. Send out invitations detailing date, time, location and where to send a reply. Keep a list of those invited and record the replies. Make sure that if it is a surprise party the invitation mentions this. Before planning a surprise party it may be advisable to try and find out discreetly whether the person for whom the party is planned would welcome this.

If as grandparents you are the chief organisers of such an event remember the following:

- plan well in advance
- stay calm
- and most importantly – **delegate!**

CHECKLIST

- List five things that you think it is necessary to do if you are minding a small grandchild.

- Make a list of some of your local places of interest which you could take your grandchildren to visit.

- What supplies would you take on a family holiday?

CASE STUDIES

Beryl looks after her grandson

Beryl is 59 and widowed. She had recently retired from her job as a clerk to nurse her husband through his last months. It eased her lonely days to see her son and his partner, Julie and their three-year-old son, Paul. When Julie was offered a part-time job, she asked Beryl if she would mind looking after her grandson. Beryl knew that Julie's income would be a great help in that household, and she agreed.

Beryl was wise enough to consult an old friend of hers, whose daughter was a nursery nurse. She was given helpful information on how to go about organising Paul's time with her. He was brought to her each day by her son, and she had a special hook put up in the passage, which was low enough for Paul to reach up and put his coat on. He had breakfast before he arrived, but mid-morning, after he had played with his toys, or drawn pictures for Beryl, they had a drink together. Beryl used this as a time when she got to know the little boy more. They had lunch at the same time each day, and most afternoons Paul had a rest, which helped Beryl too, as she could put her feet up for a while. They sometimes had a walk in the morning, or if not, Beryl made sure that she took Paul out to the nearby park later on. She encouraged him to wash his hands before meals, and after using the toilet. He was a happy little fellow. He liked to look at his books, and Beryl encouraged him to do this.

By the time a place was available at the local nursery school, Paul was well prepared, and was a well-adjusted little boy.

Keith plans a family holiday

Sybil and Keith who are 58 and 60 respectively enjoy having their families to stay. They have a large family, and now they are retired, they have much more time to enjoy them all. They had always lived in a quiet country town, which had suited the family when the children were small. Now that the grandchildren were older they wanted more entertainment. Keith had a good income and usually treated the family to the main holiday of the year.

Last year Keith decided to book a large cottage for the whole family. He had taken up golf and was pleased that the cottage was very near a well-known golf course. He told Sybil about his plans for long days on the course: 'Then home for a bath, hear all the family news and enjoy a meal together. We could have some walks on the beach if I'm not too tired.'

It was a disappointing holiday. Although Sybil had planned for bad weather, taking piles of books, puzzles *etc*, it rained almost throughout the holiday. Her daughter and son-in-law had taken their own two children, together with the children of Sybil and Keith's other daughter, who had been unable to come. The youngsters and all the children had set off each day together with the two dogs in order to try and give Sybil and Keith some space. No one had planned any menus, so Sybil had to do the shopping, and prepare an evening meal. She also had more washing and drying to do, as there were lots of muddy clothes and towels lying around.

The weather did brighten up a bit at the end of the holiday and Keith took Sybil out. However, as she told him on the way: 'It wasn't exactly a holiday, more a survival test, and next year we shall plan it better.'

Joan has her granddaughter to stay

Joan Santon, is a happy outward-going young 60-year-old. She and her husband Charlie retired several years ago and went to live in a seaside town. Charlie died soon after they moved. Joan, however made a lot of friends in the area, and so stayed there. She has two sons and one daughter, as well as several grandchildren. None of the family live near her, so each year in the holidays one or other of the grandchildren come to stay with her and they thoroughly enjoy themselves. There had never been any problems but recently when her youngest granddaughter, Lucy came to stay she was homesick.

Lucy, is just six and a half years old. She had wanted to stay with her grandmother for a few days to show that she was as grown up as the other children in her family. Her mother had thought that she might be too young, but Joan and Lucy got on very well and the little girl really seemed to be looking forward to her visit. In fact, Lucy packed her own clothes and toys, and went off with Joan quite happily.

Just before they left, Joan very wisely, asked Lucy's mum to give her some photographs of the rest of the family. 'As many recent ones as you can spare,' she told her daughter.

These came in very handy, when that night just as Lucy was getting ready for bed she began to feel homesick. When she started to cry, Joan comforted her, and told her that she was going to put all the pictures round the room so that everyone would be near her.

Joan pinned the pictures all round the small room, and even stuck a few on the curtains and bedhead. After a while, a drink, and a cuddle, Lucy settled down. Next day she asked if the pictures could stay on the walls. They did, and she went to bed quite happily that night, after she'd spoken to her mother on the phone, and told her all about the pictures.

DISCUSSION POINTS

1. How well do you think you could cope with a teenager's moods?

2. Do you think a routine is necessary if you are minding a grandchild?

3. How much planning would you give to a family holiday?

4. How do you cope with a resentful or angry grandchild while they are staying in your house?

7
Sharing a Home

This chapter looks at some of the advantages and disadvantages of either sharing your home with one or more members of your family or going to live with them. Either of these situations require a large amount of readjustment for both parties. Hopefully, however, with plenty of open discussion and sound planning the advantages will outweigh the disadvantages. Here we consider the following:

- deciding to share
- how to retain your independence
- adjusting to another home
- adapting your home for grandchildren
- sharing a home with a friend or relative
- avoiding conflicts.

DECIDING TO SHARE

There are many reasons why grandparents, children and grand-children live together; it may prove beneficial to all to share a home. Consider whether any of the following reasons would motivate you to share a home:

- financial security
- children and grandchildren have no permanent home of their own
- a single parent needs your help
- you are getting too frail to manage household chores
- you have a large house which you could share with a student grandchild.

Before making such a big decision:

1. Allow plenty of time to discuss the idea of sharing a home.

2. Make sure the change of home is a financially suitable arrangement for *all* concerned.

3. Make sure that every aspect of the proposed change is *agreed* upon.

4. If in any doubt about *any* aspect, seek legal advice.

5. Be aware that any move will take time to adjust to.

GIVING UP YOUR INDEPENDENCE

Does the thought of giving up your independence worry you? If you are in reasonably good health and are living or thinking about living with one or more members of your family you can ensure against losing your independence by having:

- a room of your own
- your own phone and personal number
- freedom and space to entertain your own friends.

Moving the family in with you

Another consideration is that you stay in your home and relatives move in with you. Whatever you decide to do it is important to consider carefully whether it is a viable financial proposition from your point of view. Take legal advice and have an agreement drawn up about rent, running costs and council tax *etc.*

If you rent rather than own your own home you may not be allowed to sub-let. Check with the following:

- the landlord
- a solicitor
- your local housing authority.

No matter how close you are to your children and grandchildren it is important to avoid any problems which may cause resentment to build up.

1. Don't allow yourself to be used for childminding or housework more often than your strength, health or energy will allow.

2. Don't make excessive demands on each other's time.

3. Guard your own privacy and respect theirs.

ADJUSTING TO ANOTHER HOME

Leaving the home you have lived in for a long time is always a wrench from the past and all your memories. You may choose to move for any number of reasons including the following:

(a) Your home is now too large for you to maintain.

(b) You think that sheltered housing might suit your requirements better than living alone.

(c) Your family have made room for you in their house.

(d) You are moving in with a relative or friend for companionship.

(d) You are going to live abroad.

Whatever your reasons try to be positive about the move. Consider how relieved you will be to have someone on hand if you are unwell, or how much the move will help you financially.

Moving in with friends or relatives

If you plan to move in with a friend or relatives there are a number of things that should be discussed beforehand:

- all aspects of the financial arrangements, *eg* sharing of bills and maintenance *etc*
- sharing the domestic chores
- having your own room
- keeping noise (radio and television) to a minimum
- sharing the garden, particularly if gardening is your great love.

After the move

Once the move has gone through, then you can begin to adjust to your new surroundings. At first, things might seem a little strange. Even the different sound of water trickling through pipes, and a door or window frame that creaks are noticeable until they become familiar.

ADAPTING YOUR HOME FOR GRANDCHILDREN

It is not uncommon for grandparents to have their grandchildren living with them. Often, this is because their son or daughter is a single parent and it is a practical, as well as a caring solution to the problem of where a family should live. It can also be a help to a parent if they are working or studying, because if grandparents are willing, they can mind their grandchildren. Living together as two families can sometimes, however, be claustrophobic but steps can be taken to make things run smoothly.

- Decide how housework/shopping/cooking *etc* can be divided equally.

- Where a baby is sharing your home make sure you have some part of the day to yourself.

- Be helpful, but avoid being taken for granted.

- Try not to criticise how your grandchildren are dressed/brought up *etc*.

- If possible have separate rooms.

Making more room
You may be lucky enough to have a large house, in which case you may be able to adapt rooms so that you are each self-contained. If your home is smaller however, it is essential for you all to discuss matters like:

1. The mealtime and bedtime routine.

2. The shared use of the kitchen and bathroom.

3. The importance of respecting each other's privacy.

Reaching an understanding
If you have a teenager living in your home, you will most likely find that the television and telephone are used more often. This is fine providing you come to some understanding about the financial arrangements regarding these.

You may live in a house or flat which is in close proximity to your neighbours. You will have to explain to the children the need to keep the noise level down.

Another point often overlooked is the garden area. You may have a garden and lawn that you take pride in but naturally, any grandchildren living with you will want to use this as a play area.

State openly *before* they move in how you feel about this, and discuss other arrangements such as:

- using a hard concrete area for ball games
- using a soft ball for some games
- playing ball in the local park and not in the garden.

SHARING A HOME WITH A RELATIVE OR FRIEND

You may be lonely, or a relative or friend may have suggested you share a home. Such a decision requires long and careful consideration and discussion. Ask yourself the following questions:

(a) Is your home suitable for sharing with someone else?

(b) How would the financial arrangements be worked out?

(c) Could you live in someone else's home?

(d) How would you feel about having to get rid of some of your furniture?

Give yourself plenty of time to consider all these things (and more). After all, you are probably talking about sharing for the rest of your life with this person so think hard before committing yourself. You will not only be sharing your *home*, but in a way, your life.

Sharing with someone older

If you are thinking of sharing with a friend or relative who is the same age or older than you consider the problems that may arise as one of you becomes frail and more dependent on the other. Make enquiries from your social services department and your GP about what help would be available in this situation. This could include:

- home care
- meals-on-wheels
- short-term respite care in a local home or hospital.

Keeping some privacy

You may be worried that you will lose your privacy if you share your home with someone, even if it is a close friend or relative. There are ways however, of enjoying the benefits of sharing a home whilst at the same time guarding your privacy.

1. Divide your property into two flats, if it is viable both from a financial and practical point of view.

2. Have a room of your own. It may be possible to divide a large sitting room into two smaller ones.

3. Think about installing an extra toilet and/or shower room somewhere in the house.

4. Ensure that you have your own space and time when necessary.

It is important to make sure that the companionship you gain by sharing a home is balanced by the occasional need to be able to enjoy your own company.

AVOIDING CONFLICTS

There are bound to be potential areas of conflict when sharing a house. Two people sharing a kitchen for example, can easily lead to conflict. It may be possible to arrange a rota for either using the kitchen independently or to make sure that the chores are evenly shared.

Children too, can unintentionally cause conflict between adults especially when standards of behaviour and tidiness do not coincide. This is an area which needs discussion and compromise but try and avoid the following:

1. **Criticising** children's behaviour without telling the parents.

2. **Grumbling and nagging** a child if you object to something they have done or said.

3. **Lending money** to the grandchildren unless there is a very good reason and certainly not behind the parents' backs.

4. **Criticising** children's table manners whilst sharing a family meal. Discuss manners with the parents if you feel they need improving but don't let mealtimes become stressful times.

5. **Taking sides** in an argument within the family.

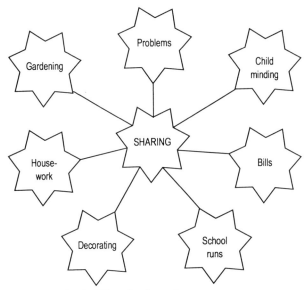

Fig. 9. What sharing a home can mean.

Whether sharing a home with a friend or family, conflicts are bound to arise. None of us is perfect and we all have small irritating habits. We do not like these being brought to our attention so neither should we do that to those we live with.

Ultimately however, in spite of the potential problems of sharing a home it can provide companionship and support for all concerned. See Figure 9.

CASE STUDIES

Ellen and her daughter-in-law share the chores

Ellen aged 59 had lived in the same small country town all her life. She and her husband Alf lived in a bungalow with a large garden on the edge of town. When their son who lived in another area, was made redundant and had his home repossessed he and his wife and three-year-old son came to live with Ellen and Alf.

All went well for the first two months, although the bungalow did seem overcrowded at times. Fortunately their son managed to get work after a while, and this meant that he was not in the bungalow during the daytime which made things a little easier. Because her son and his wife had lived some distance away Ellen had not got to know her daughter-in-law very well. They had only met infrequently on family occasions.

This being the case, Ellen thought it wise to have an open discussion about coping with housework, meals, shopping *etc*. Ellen has a set routine for washing which she did on the same two days each week. She suggested that her daughter-in-law used the washing machine and the tumble dryer on the other days. They also decided to alternate on the cooking, one week each. Alf had always helped out with housework, and this he continued to do.

This arrangement was a great help for both women. Shopping lists were drawn up by both of them well in advance of a weekly shop. The bungalow had three roomy bedrooms so the little boy used his as a playroom also. Ellen's son and wife had their own television in their bedroom.

Having planned and discussed things so well meant that there were only a few minor irritations to cope with. They were all still on good terms when Ellen's son and family eventually moved into a rented flat.

Catherine loses a friend

Catherine was left with a large house when she was widowed. She enjoyed her home and garden, and although she did not have any close family, she had several good friends. At 70, she was still very active, and grew most of her own vegetables, some of which won prizes. However, she did find that the cost of running the house was draining her savings, so she was keen to accept her old friend Marjorie's suggestion, that she move in and help out with both the work and the running costs.

Once Marjorie had moved in Catherine realised that she hadn't given enough thought to what it all entailed. Firstly, they have never discussed the sharing of household bills. Marjorie had been horrified to find that the council tax and water rates were much higher than she had been paying. Catherine worried about this, and agreed to pay more than half these bills herself.

The second problem was the fact that Marjorie had several noisy grandchildren who visited her regularly. Two of these were teenagers, and on several occasions had played loud music whilst in the garden. It was when they kicked a football about on Catherine's prized vegetable garden, trampling produce underfoot, that she confronted her friend by telling her that her grandchildren were inconsiderate and rude. This caused an argument, and Marjorie left the house. Catherine gained nothing by sharing her home, and also lost a good friend.

Frank resolves a conflict

Frank is a 68-year-old widower. After his wife died a year ago, he found that his large house was too much for him to manage. It made sense therefore, for his son David, who had just been divorced to go and live with him. Although Frank's ex-daughter-in-law had custody of their ten-year-old son, he came and stayed with his father regularly. 'Will this be OK?' David asked Frank, who had no hesitation in telling him that of course it was. Frank was fond of his grandson Adrian, and indeed he had been fond of his daughter-in-law, and was upset when she and David had divorced. After David moved in he and Frank discussed the possibility of having the property converted into two flats.

The work on the conversion into two flats seemed to drag on. However, although Frank was tired because of the extra clearing up involved he enjoyed the company of his son. He especially enjoyed it when his grandson came to stay. The building work was finished and the decorators moved in. The house became more orderly, although there was still a lot to do. At about this time David began seeing a woman he worked with. 'You'll like her Dad,' he told his father.

However, when David brought her home Frank was disappointed. She was nothing like his ex-daughter-in-law, but she did get on well with young Adrian. She often took him out for treats such as the cinema. She was also a karate expert, which was something that interested Adrian. Adrian spoke of her all the time, telling his grandfather about all the things she could do. It was when Frank found that she had also given Adrian some extra pocket money that he spoke out: 'She's spoiling you, trying to take on your mother's place.' His words upset Adrian who then told his father.

The upshot was that David threatened to leave. He told his father that he had no right to speak to the boy like that, or to say the things he had about the new girlfriend. That night Frank sat alone, thinking over what he'd said. He knew that he had been wrong to interfere. Next day he apologised to David and blamed his outburst on tiredness, and possible jealousy over David's new friendship. Fortunately David had always been fond of his father, and he accepted the older man's apology.

Rose moves in with her daughter

Rose is nearly 80 and had lived in her small house for many years. Even though her eyesight was failing and she suffered from rheumatism, she was convinced that she could still manage on her own. Her two daughters and son loved their mother and were anxious about her living alone. They asked her to consider moving into suitable residential accommodation but she stubbornly refused. She had daily help and her son and other relatives helped out when they could in her garden, but it was mainly at night when they felt she was particularly at risk.

Because of her diminishing eyesight Rose's living area became confined to downstairs. The family had decided therefore, that they would pay to have a toilet and washbasin installed downstairs. However, before they could organise this Rose had a bad fall in her kitchen one morning. Fortunately the home carer found her and phoned for an ambulance. When her family visited, her eldest daughter told her: 'That's it Mum, you can't go on living alone.' To everyone's surprise Rose agreed – the fall had obviously frightened her.

When she was discharged from hospital, Rose went to live with her eldest daughter and family. They were careful to explain to her that it was only temporary so that she could see whether she liked it: 'If you feel happy with us, we could build an extension downstairs so that you have your own rooms. It would be overlooking the garden, so it would be nice and light.'

Rose wasn't put under any pressure by her daughter and began to relax and enjoy the security that sharing a home gave her. After a month she agreed to their suggestion of having the extension built. They also rented her own house, with her full agreement. The income from this helped to pay the bills in her new 'granny flat' which she insisted on paying in order to, as she put: 'Keep my independence!'

DISCUSSION POINTS

1. How much discussion do you think is necessary before deciding to share your home?

2. Which organisation would you go to for legal advice?

3. Would it help you financially to share your home with a relative or friend?

4. Do you consider it essential to have your own garden? How important is your privacy to you?

5. Do you prefer to live alone even if your home is too large to manage comfortably?

6. Would you consider moving into the home of a relative?

8
Adjusting to Your New Role

It may well be that the idea of becoming a grandparent takes a little while to get used to especially if you are still relatively young, in your early fifties or even forties. This chapter discusses some of the psychological adjustments you may have to make when you become a grandparent. These are as follows:

- facing the fact that you are now a grandparent
- accepting your new role
- learning about children
- keeping in touch
- retaining your independence.

FACING THE FACTS

Do you feel that becoming a grandparent has an ominous ring about it? – that it's the end of life as you know it? Perhaps these are some of the questions that will rush through your mind as you consider your new role.

- *Am I now one of the 'older generation'?*
  Only if you want to be – surely age or even ageing is an attitude of mind. You might find that being with young children makes you feel young and vital again.

- *Will my life be one round of endless babysitting?*
  You will simply have to learn to say 'no' if you don't wish to babysit. Being a grandparent doesn't mean being at everyone's beck and call. There are probably other grandparents, relatives and friends who are more than willing to take their turn.

- *Will I have to be called 'Granny' or 'Grandpa', which I'll hate?*
  You can decide what name you'd like to be called by your grandchildren – whatever you think is appropriate.

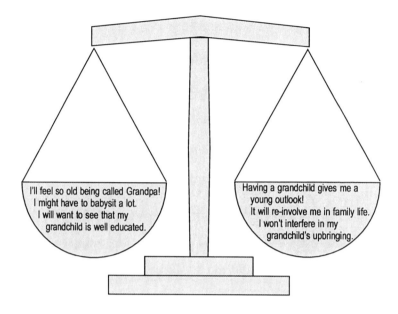

Fig. 10. Getting the balance right.

If you do have reservations about becoming a grandparent there is no need to feel guilty about it, after all it's a major milestone in your life. Talk to your children about how you feel. Discuss your feelings also with other grandparents. To meet with other grandparents why not join one of the following organisations?

- a local retirement or pre-retirement club
- a local political group
- the University of the Third Age
- the Grandparents' Federation.

Being positive
There are many positive sides to becoming a grandparent, such as:

1. The arrival of a baby can draw a daughter or son closer to their parents.

2. The welcome you give to a new baby's arrival may heal any rift there might have been in the family.

3. Becoming a grandparent offers a second chance to become a better parent.

4. Grandparenting allows you to be more involved in the life of your family.

5. Having a grandchild may revitalise you and give you a younger attitude towards life.

As with most things there is a positive and a negative side but hopefully the positive will outweigh the negative. See Figure 10.

ACCEPTING THE NEW ROLE

Once the baby is born, there is no turning the clock back. **You are now a grandparent**. Whatever your feelings about this, it has to be accepted. If you still feel unsure about this new role, try to remember the following:

(a) Grandparents who never become involved with their grand-children lose out on what could be an enriching relationship.

(b) You may be glad to find that in this new role you will be able to give practical help.

(c) As a grandparent you may be called upon to fill in as a temporary parent.

(d) You may be in a position to help your grandchild achieve the things you did not.

(e) If the parents of your grandchild divorce, or are separated for either a short- or long-term period, you may well be the person who can help your grandchild through this traumatic period.

Once you've accepted the role don't go to the other extreme and try to impose your views on how to bring the children up. It's easily done, because you are convinced that you know best. You may feel that having been a parent, you are an expert in raising children. Take care not to:

• interfere with the upbringing of your grandchildren
• criticise how the baby is fed or what time it goes to bed

- comment unsympathetically if a new mother isn't coping well or seems depressed
- insist that your grandchild is educated in a certain way.

The trick is to show that you are willing to be helpful, but to know when your advice is *not* required.

Remarrying and gaining grandchildren

You may have been widowed or divorced and have now remarried. Because of this you may have acquired a new role as a step-grandparent. These grandchildren are now part of your extended family. If it is possible, try to meet the step-grandchildren before your marriage takes place. You can arrange this by:

- having a special occasion for you all to meet
- inviting them to your home.

Make sure that you know their names, ages, schools *etc*. Remember that it is a new situation for them also. Perhaps as you get to know them better, they will help you decide what name they will call you as you slip into this new role. Be prepared to overcome some resentment. The children may be missing their natural grandparent, and have to come to terms with this. A lot of new grandparents have faced this problem and patience, tact and understanding are required on all sides.

LEARNING ABOUT CHILDREN

As a grandparent you have a chance to be a 'parent' the second time around. All those things that you are sorry you didn't know about when your own children were babies, can now come in useful. You will have had time to consider how to talk to adolescents, as well as toddlers. Most importantly, with maturity you will have learnt when *not* to intervene in some of their problems, that is, of course, unless they ask you to. Your grandchildren will, because of their education and the media, be far more aware of the sort of things that may have never been spoken of when you were younger. With older children you will learn:

1. That they speak frankly about certain subjects like sex and drugs *etc*.

2. That they are still (as ever), going through a time of growth and change in themselves.

3. They can often be under pressure and stress, due to examinations, work patterns, a break-up in family relationships and other factors.

Learning about adolescent grandchildren

You may have to work very hard to get to know how best to deal with some of the things that upset teenagers. Again, the simple act of just being there, is something that grandparents do particularly well. A comforting meal, a bed for the night, maybe a shoulder to cry on. 'Oh, Nan, you're someone we know that we can go and tell our troubles to', is the greatest compliment a grandmother could receive. Making a long distance phone call, or sending a letter showing that you care, is something that you have probably learnt to do over the years, knowing what comfort either can bring.

Learning about babies again

Something you don't have to learn about again is the joy of seeing and holding that new baby, that just comes naturally. This isn't always possible of course, but if you do not live near the family and cannot see the baby often, you can still be asking questions. This way you will learn about the baby's growth, and who it resembles of course. Dr Spock may be out of fashion, but there are many new books on babies and their development. Keep in touch with new ideas in the following ways:

(a) Read new books on caring for babies and bringing up children.

(b) Ask the baby's mother about how she copes.

(c) Offer to bath or mind the baby.

(d) Take note of how babies are dressed these days.

(e) If you live far away ask for regular photos to be sent so that you can see how baby is growing.

Getting to know about toddlers

All children are different of course, but there are certain stages that little ones go through. Did you know all about these different stages when you were bringing up your own children? As parents ourselves we did what we thought was right when coping with a tantrum, or a crying session, or a child who wouldn't sleep. When your grandchildren are toddlers they may have similar sessions, but at different times and perhaps for different reasons. So accept that sometimes these things will happen, and get to know about them in the following ways:

1. By offering to look after your grandchild when you know this would be welcomed.

2. By taking your grandchild out alone.

3. By having the family to stay.

4. By asking your grandchild's parents how they cope.

Remember, that most of these little traumas are part and parcel of a child's development. Continue to play with your grandchild, and read to them whenever possible. Watch them grow, and enjoy every minute that they spend with you.

Keeping in touch

It is important to maintain links in families. As has been mentioned earlier, even if a family is separated and divided, grandparents are allowed access to see their grandchildren. If there has been a separation in the family tackle the problem of keeping in touch head-on:

(a) Maintain contact with all parties if there is a divorce or separation that could divide you from your grandchildren.

(b) Obtain legal help if necessary.

(c) Join the Grandparents' Federation.

(d) Try in every amicable way first to see your grandchildren.

(e) Make your home a place where comfort and support are given.

Moving away

In retirement grandparents often move away from the family in order perhaps to live by the sea, or in the country. If you decide to move, make sure you are the person who always writes and/or telephones regularly. Have the grandchildren come and visit you, they will enjoy using your house as their 'second home'.

If you live near your grandchildren, or have moved nearer to them, then you may have opportunities to see them more often. As children get older they lead busy lives. School work takes up a lot of their time and they will have friends and clubs and activities that keep them occupied. However, you can still keep in touch in the following ways:

1. Attend school functions *eg* concerts, sports days, prizegiving *etc*.

2. If your home is en route for any of their activities ask them to call in now and then. Explain that they do not have to stop long, and that their friends can accompany them.

3. Go and watch them in that all-important football, cricket or netball match. Or any other fixture that your grandchildren may be taking part in.

4. Show your concern by telephoning if any of your grandchildren are unwell.

5. Always have time to talk to your grandchildren.

RETAINING YOUR INDEPENDENCE

You might sometimes feel that you are losing your independence by assuming the all-important role of grandparent. This will inevitably happen if you constantly make yourself available to do the following:

1. Babysit at any time you are asked to.

2. Have the grandchildren for long periods during school holidays.

3. Do shopping/washing and general household chores every day for the family.

4. Drive your grandchildren to and from school on a regular basis.

5. Give up your own activities and hobbies to help out with the grandchildren.

Obviously, as a caring grandparent you will always want to help out if necessary, and especially in any sort of emergency.

Maybe you are helping a lone parent bring up your grandchild and you will probably be quite happy about this. Make sure though, that you allow yourself time for some of your own activities. This way, by having time out for your club, or some other interest, you will recover your energy as well as retain your independence.

The need for independence

Helping out as grandparents is part of our role, and most of us accept this as natural. However, we are still individuals, and will have created areas in our lives in order to enjoy hobbies or use our particular talents. Make sure that you do not take on commitments within the family which prevent you from following your own interests. These may include:

- hobbies
- voluntary work
- sporting activities
- holidays.

You can still take part in all of these whilst still being able to see your family on a regular basis, or help out with your grandchildren when asked. Of course, if there is a time when someone is ill in your family, your help and support may well be needed for longer periods. Other interests and hobbies can be put aside until things improve, or until another routine is worked out, or other people lend a hand.

QUESTIONS AND ANSWERS

My new step-grandson is thirteen years old. I find it very difficult to relate to him, as I never had a son of my own. His interests seem mainly to be sport, and the latest pop songs. How should I talk to him?

Be patient. Let him do the talking at first if he wants to. Do compliment him if he has won something at any particular sport, and try to learn the names of some of today's pop stars. Mention any sport you are interested in and ask him what he thinks about some famous sports person. Lead him into a conversation like this, but do not try too hard or he will think you are merely being condescending.

I have been told by my daughter that I am to become a grandmother. I hate the idea, it makes me appear to be so old. I am in my fifties, still working and very active. I am concerned that I will be asked to babysit a lot. What can I do to overcome these negative feelings about being a grandmother?

What you are hating is the idea of old age. Surely this is an attitude of mind? Some 80 and 90-year-olds are still very active, and they are probably grandparents too. There is no question of you having to give up your work or any of your activities. Say before the baby is born, that you feel you would not make a good babysitter. You may find that once the baby is born, that you have a different outlook entirely, and will be quite happy to mind your grandchild.

My son and his wife have a little boy of two. They seem to spoil him a lot. They do not chastise him when he removes ornaments from a shelf. They let him eat sweets, and if he wakes in the night they take him into their bed. I feel that all of this is wrong, and the child will not be helped by their attitude. How can I make them see that what they are doing is not right for my grandson?

You should say nothing. You are not the parent of the child, and it is the parents that are responsible for his upbringing. At the age of two a child is discovering what happens in his little world. Removing ornaments shows curiousity and not vandalism. It is the parents who make all the decisions. As long as the child is healthy and not abused in any way, then you will have to accept that you can enjoy watching him grow, but must remain silent about how he is brought up.

CHECKLIST

- List five good things about becoming a grandparent.

- List some ways in which you think grandparenting can give you a young attitude.

- Consider some ways in which you will make a better grandparent than you did a parent.

CASE STUDIES

Lynn has a change of heart

Lynn was shattered to learn that she was to become a grandmother. A divorcée, not quite 50, she resented the fact of being thought of as old. Her daughter Penny was unmarried, and living in a couple of rooms in the town where her boyfriend was studying for a degree in engineering. 'What a mess,' Lynn told her friends. 'Baby smells, baby cries and broken nights.' She dreaded the thought of it all.

When her grandson was born, Lynn did not visit for a few days. When she did call the baby was asleep and Lynn couldn't believe the tug of love she felt when she saw him. She wouldn't wait for him to wake, but lifted him straight away. Holding him close, she told her daughter: 'You know, I almost feel that I could feed him if I had to, the upsurge of emotion I feel is so great.'

After the first meeting Lynn could not do enough for her daughter and grandson. She often remarked that it was like being a mum second time round.

Maud tries to impose her views

Maud and Jack, a couple in their seventies, had a large family, including grandchildren. However, none of these lived near them. Only their son John and his partner lived in their area, and they had no children.

Maud had reconciled herself to being a long-distance grand-mother, when she was delighted to hear from John that his partner was to have a baby. 'And you're so near,' she told him. When a baby girl was born she made and knitted baby clothes which she took round. John's partner thanked her politely, but Maud noticed after a while, that she never saw the baby in any of these clothes. One day, she questioned her son about this, and looking very embarrassed he told her that his partner had thought that they weren't up-to-date enough. 'You mean she thinks they're old-fashioned', said Maud who was upset and angry.

Maud and Jack were lucky with their son and family living so near. They were often invited round for a meal, but Maud was still upset about the baby-clothes she had made, and made constant reference to what babies wore nowadays. She would make remarks such as: 'Babies are put in all sorts of unsuitable clothes nowadays, they must feel the cold poor little things', or 'Shop bought clothes never last the amount of washing they go through.'

Maud persisted with this attitude. She also made other

derogatory remarks about her grandchild's upbringing.

After a time they were not invited round to their son's home very much and soon the invitations stopped altogether. Again Maud was upset but Jack told her that she had only herself to blame. Eventually, it was Jack who talked to his son and partner. Whatever was said did ease the situation, although there is still a certain coolness between the two women. Maud regrets the things she said, and is trying hard to keep a good relationship going with her son's partner so that she doesn't miss out on watching her granddaughter grow up.

Phyllis tries hard to overcome Emma's resentment

Phyllis is in her early sixties, and has been divorced for some years. She had no children. It was at the local dramatic society of which she was a keen member that she had met Graham who had recently joined. They got on well straight away, and after going out for a while decided that they would get married. Phyllis was delighted to know that she would be acquiring a 'ready-made family'. Graham was widowed and had three children: two sons, and a daughter who was married with two teenagers, a boy and a girl. Phyllis met them all at family gatherings, but never had long enough with any of them to get to know them very well. She was pleased that Graham had grandchildren, because it was something she had always wanted.

After the wedding, Phyllis moved into Graham's large house. Once a week one of his sons would call round. His daughter came several times, with her husband and Graham's granddaughter. The girl, Emma, was polite but very distant towards Phyllis. On Saturdays she attended ballet class near to Graham's house. She would call in afterwards and Graham would drive her home.

Phyllis suggested to Graham that Emma stayed to have a meal with them. As she was 14, Phyllis thought it might make her feel grown up and she also hoped that by doing this she would get to know her step-granddaughter better. However, Emma was sullen and withdrawn when she did come for a meal.

Phyllis's step-grandson was quite friendly and told them about his friends and the football team he played for. Phyllis decided therefore, that it was best to say nothing and just hope that Emma would come to like her.

One day Emma called to collect her school bag which she'd left behind. Graham was out and when Emma realised this she turned to go. Phyllis asked her: 'Why won't you stay?' 'Because you are *not* my grandmother, and you will never take her place,' she screamed as she rushed out. Phyllis was in tears when Graham returned.

Through a friend Phyllis heard about an association called 'Stepfamily' which provides a helpline, together with publications about becoming a step-grandparent. Phyllis felt cheered by the fact that she could talk to someone who understood. A free information pack from this organisation proved valuable.

Graham was supportive, and decided to sell his old home with all its old memories. They remained in the same town but in new property. This gave everyone a fresh start. Gradually as Emma got older and more involved with examinations, and the prospects of going to university, she began to relate to Phyllis in a better way.

DISCUSSION POINTS

1. Do you consider yourself to be a second parent now that you are a grandparent?

2. Would you think it necessary to make any comment if your baby grandchild cried a lot?

3. What advice do you think you should give about the education of your grandchild?

4. How would you react if a step-grandchild made it obvious that they resented you?

5. How important do you think it is to get to know your step-grandchildren?

6. Would you be aware if a grandchild was suffering from stress?

Further Reading

ALCOHOL PROBLEMS
Alcohol, Dr Gerald Beales (Daniels, 1994, Quick Guide Series).
Alcohol Facts 10–14 years, Dr Gerald Beales (Daniels, 1994, Quick Guide Series).

BEREAVEMENT

Badger's Parting Gifts, Susan Varley (Anderson Press, 1976).
Dealing with a Death in the Family, Sylvia Murphy (How To Books, 1997).
Grandpa, John Burningham, (Jonathan Cape, 1984).
Grandpa and Me, Marlee and Benny Alex (Lion Publishing, 1981).
Helping Children Cope with Grief, Rosemary Wells (Sheldon Press, 1988).

BULLYING

Bullying: A Practical Guide to Coping, Michele Elliott (Harlow, Longman, 1991).
Bullying at school, Dan Olweus (Blackwell, 1993).
Bullysaurus, Damon Burnard (Hodder, 1996).
Helping Children Cope with Bullying, Sarah Lawson (Sheldon, 1994).

DRUG AND SOLVENT PROBLEMS

D – mag, Julian Cohen and edited by Harry Shapiro (Institute for the Study of Drug Dependence, 1995).
Drugs and Solvents You and Your Child, based on a text written by TACADE (The Advisory Council on Alcohol and Drug Education 1994). Produced by the Central Office of Information on behalf of the Department of Health. This, and a wide range of similar booklets, available free from BAPS, Health Publications Unit,

DSS Distribution Centre, Heywood Stores, Manchester Road, Heywood, Lancashire OL10 2PZ or phone free. Tel: 0800 555 777.

Drugs Education 4–11 Years, Janice Slough (Daniels, 1994).

Drugs Education 11–16 Years, Janice Slough (Daniels, 1994).

Solvents Drugs and Young People, Richard Ives and Barbara Wyvill (Daniels, 1994).

GENERAL

Bertie Visits Grannie, Paddy Bouma (Bodley Head, 1987).

Families Matter, in Association with the National Family Trust, Richard Whitfield (Marshall Pickering, 1987).

Gran and Granpa, Helen Oxenbury (Walker Books, 1984).

Grandma, Debbie Bailey (Annick Press, 1994).

Grandpa, Debbie Bailey (Annick Press, 1994).

The Granny Project, Anne Fine (Methuen, 1983).

Your Grandchild and You, Rosemary Wells (Sheldon Press, 1990). Available in large print (Isis, 1991).

ONE PARENT FAMILIES

How to Help, A Guide for Family and Friends of Lone parents, (One Parent Families Publications, 1995). Available from the National Council for One Parent Familes, 255 Kentish Town Road, London NW5 2LX.

Successful Single Parenting, Mike Lilley (How To Books, 1996).

PREMATURE BIRTH

Born Too Early, Pete Moore (Thorsons, 1995). Available from all good bookshops or by sending £5.99 to Action Research, Vincent House, Horsham, West Sussex RH12 2DP.

SEXUALITY

Where Do I Come From?, Claire Rayner (Arlington, 1989).

The Body Book, Claire Rayner (Pan Books, 1979).

Growing Pains and How to Avoid Them, Claire Rayner (Heinemann, 1984).

Life Love and Everything, Children's Questions Answered, Claire Rayner (Kylie Cathie, 1993).

STEP FAMILIES

Katie Morag and the Two Grandmothers, Mairi Hedderwick (Bodley Head, 1985).

The Not So Wicked Stepmother, Lizi Boyd (Viking Kestrel, 1988).

Stepfamilies, Karen Bryant-Mole (Wayland Publishers Ltd, 1993).

Two More Steps: Reflections on Stepgrandparenting, Donna Smith and Margaret Robinson (National Stepfamily Association Publications, 1996). Available from the Association at: 3rd Floor, Chapel House, 18 Hatton Place, London EC1N 8RU.

Useful Addresses

CHILD ABDUCTION

Childrens' Legal Centre, 20 Compton Terrace, London N1 2LN.
Tel: (01206) 873 820.

International Social Services, Cranmer House, 39 Brixton Road,
London SW9 6DD. Tel: (0171) 735 8941.

The Lord Chancellor's Department, 81 Chancery Lane, London
WC2A 1DD. Tel: (0171) 911 7047.

Reunite National Council for Abducted Children, PO Box 4,
London WC1X 3DX. Tel: Advice Line (0171) 404 8356.

CHILDREN IN CARE

Family Rights Group, The Print House, 18 Ashwin Street, London
E8 3DL. Tel: (0171) 923 2628.

Grandparents' Federation, Moot House, The Stowe, Harlow, Essex
CM20 3AG. Tel: (01279) 444964.

HOLIDAY HELP

Family Holiday Association, Hertford Lodge, East End Road,
London N3 3QE. Tel: (0181) 349 4044. To provide holidays to
under-privileged families.

Holiday Care Service, 2nd Floor, Imperial Buildings, Victoria
Road, Horley, Surrey RH6 7PZ. Tel: (01293) 774535. A holiday
information service which gives free advice to anyone who,
because of disability or other special needs or family circumstances, has difficulty in finding a suitable holiday.

Holiday Endeavour for Lone Parents (HELP), 57 Owston Road,
Carcroft, Doncaster DN6 8DA. Tel: (01302) 726959. To provide
low-cost holidays for single parent families in Great Britain.

Holidays One-Parents (HOP), 51 Hampshire Road, Droylsden,
Manchester M43 7PH. Tel: (0161) 370 0337.

Scout Holiday Homes Trust, Baden-Powell House, Queen's Gate, London SW7 5JS. Tel: (0171) 584 7030. To provide affordable self-catering holidays for families with a handicapped member or with special needs. No scouting connection necessary.

Send a Child to Hucklow Fund, 41 Bradford Drive, Ewell, Epsom, Surrey KT19 0AQ. Tel: (0181) 393 9122. To arrange and administer holidays at the Unitarian Holiday Centre, Gt Hucklow, for needy and deprived children without regard to religious, political, racial and other considerations.

ONE PARENT FAMILIES

National Council for One Parent Families, 255 Kentish Town Road, London NW5 2LX. Tel: (0171) 267 1361.

PREMATURE BIRTH

Action Research, Vincent House, Horsham, West Sussex RH12 2DP. Tel: (01403) 210406.

STEPFAMILIES

National Stepfamily Association, 3rd Floor, Chapel House, 18 Hatton Place, London EC1N 8RU. Tel: (0171) 209 2464.

USEFUL ASSOCIATIONS AND SOCIETIES

Action for Blind People, 14 Verney Road, London SE16. Tel: (0171) 732 8771.

Benefit Enquiry Line for general advice regarding Social Security Benefit for disabled people, Room 800a, Victoria House, Ormskirk Road, Preston PR1 2QP. Freephone: 0800 88 22 00.

Both Parents Forever, 39 Cloonmore Avenue, Orpington, Kent BR6 9LE. Tel: (01689) 854343. (To help all parents, grandparents and children understand their rights following divorce, separation or care proceedings, and to help them obtain their rights, amicably if possible, or through court proceedings if necessary.)

Children need Grandparents, 2 Surrey Way, Laindon West, Basildon, Essex SS15 6PS. Tel: (01268) 414607. (To offer mutual aid and advice to grandparents who are refused access to their grandchildren.)

The Children's Society, Edward Rudolf House, Margery Street, London WC1X 0JL. Tel: (0171) 837 4299.

Dial UK (Supports UK-wide disability information and advice services), St Catherine's Hospital, Park Lodge, Tickhill Road, Balby, Doncaster DN4 8QN. Tel: (01302) 310123.

Disability Alliance Educational and Research Association, Universal House, 88–94 Wentworth Street, London E1 7SA. Tel: (0171) 247 8776. (Advice line: (0171) 247 8763.)

Disability Law Service, Room 241, 49–51 Bedford Row, London WC1R 4LR. Tel: (0171) 831 8031.

Families Anonymous is a self-help group for parents of drug users, and has branches in various parts of the country. Tel: (0171) 498 4680 for further details.

Family Action Information and Rescue (FAIR) 1976, BCM Box 3535, PO Box 12, London WC1N 3XX. Tel: (0181) 539 3940. (Advice for families information/education concerned with young people in extreme religious cults.) Helpline (01482) 443104.

Family Crisis Line, c/o Ashwood House, Ashwood Road, Woking, Surrey GU22 7JW. Tel: (01483) 722533 (10am to 10pm daily).

Families Need Fathers, 134 Curtain Road, London EC2A 3AR. Tel: (0181) 886 0970 (information line). Advice and support for separating and divorcing parents to ensure their children maintain contact (including unmarried parents).

The Lady Hoare Trust for Physically Disabled Children, Mitre House, 44–46 Fleet Street, London EC4Y 1BN. Tel: (0171) 583 1951.

National Benevolent Fund for the Aged, 1 Leslie Grove Place, Croydon CRO 6TJ. Tel: (0181) 688 6655. To provide direct help to improve the quality of life for older people.

National Childbirth Trust, Alexander House, Oldham Terrace, London W3 6NH. Tel: (0181) 992 8637. Offers information and support in pregnancy, childbirth and early parenthood, and to enable all parents to make informed choices.

National Council for the Divorced and Separated, 13 High Street, Little Shelford, Cambridge CB2 5ES. Tel: (0116) 2700 595.

The National Deafblind and Rubella Association (SENSE), 11-13 Clifton Terrace, London N4 3SR. Tel: (0171) 272 7774.

The National Deaf Children's Society, 15 Dufferin Street, London EC1V 8PD. Tel: (0171) 250 0123.

National Drugs Helpline, PO Box 5000, Glasgow G12 9JQ. Freephone: (0800) 77 66 00.

The National Family Trust, 101 Queen Victoria Street, London

EC4P 4EP. Tel: (01242) 251583.

RADAR (The Royal Associaton for Disability and Rehabilitation), 12 City Forum, 250 City Road, London EC1V 8AF. Tel: (0171) 250 3222.

Royal National Institute for the Blind, 224 Great Portland Street, London W1N 6AA. Tel: (0171) 388 1266.

Royal National Institute for Deaf People (RNID), 105 Gower Street, London WC1E 6AH. Tel: (0171) 387 8033.

The Snowdon Award Scheme, 22 Horsham Court, 6 Brighton Road, Horsham, West Sussex RH13 5BA. Tel: (01403) 211252.

University of the Third Age, National Office, 1 Stockwell Green, London SW9. Tel: (0171) 837 8838.

Index